RANGERS F.C.

- THE 25 YEAR RECORD

1970-71 to 1994-95 Seasons

SEASON BY SEASON WRITE-UPS
David Powter

EDITOR
Michael Robinson

CONTENTS

British Library Cataloguing in Publication Data
A catalogue record for this book is available from the British Library
ISBN 0-947808-68-X

Printed by Redwood Books, Kennet House, Kennet Way, Trowbridge, Wilts.

RANGERS F.C.
- Seasons 1970-71 to 1994-95

During the 25 seasons which ended in May 1995, Rangers were the most successful club in British football. They won six more trophies than England's premier side, Liverpool, secured in the same period; and ten more than their great rivals, Celtic. The Gers' haul was 11 Scottish League titles, 7 Scottish Cups, 11 League Cups and the 1971-72 European Cup Winners' Cup. Their title successes in 1974-75 and 1986-87 came after the Ibrox fans had waited impatiently for 11 and 9 seasons, respectively. Conversely, the 1994-95 Championship success was the club's seventh on the trot.

Yet back in October 1970, Rangers had gone five barren seasons before the trophy cabinet was dusted to make room for the League Cup. A single goal by 16 year old Derek Johnstone was enough to wrest the cup away from Celtic, winners for the previous 5 years.

Johnstone was on the mark again in the drawn Scottish Cup final against the same opponents the following May. Celtic gifted an own-goal in the replay but that was their only moment of generosity as the Gers had to be content with runners-up medals. The three Hampden Park Cup finals between the two Glasgow clubs attracted a massive aggregate of 329,000 spectators.

Willie Waddell's side fell to Bayern Munich at the first hurdle in the UEFA Cup. Their prospects had appeared bright after the first 90 minutes when they trailed by just a solitary Beckenbauer goal. However, the return leg at Ibrox ended 1-1 and the Germans went through on aggregate.

Willie Johnston bagged the Gers' goal in that UEFA Cup tie, and he and record signing Colin Stein were the club's joint top League scorers, with 11 goals. After finishing as runners-up to Celtic on the previous 5 occasions, Rangers slipped to 4th place in 1970-71 as the Celts regained the crown in front of Aberdeen and St Johnstone.

Dave Smith was voted 'Player of the Year' by the Scottish Football Writers' Association as Rangers moved up to third 12 months later, but again made little impression on Celtic (or Aberdeen). They lost 4 of their first 5 games including the home fixtures with their two main rivals.

Celtic also put paid to the Gers' hopes of retaining the League Cup by winning both meetings in the early group games to ensure that they, and not Rangers, progressed to the quarter-finals. Rangers' last hope of winning a domestic trophy in 1971-72 disappeared when they were beaten 2-0 in a Scottish Cup semi-final replay by Hibs. However, that was far from the end of their season as they progressed to the final of the European Cup Winners' Cup.

After defeating Stade Rennes in the first round, Waddell's men side-stepped Sporting Lisbon on away goals after two high scoring matches. Rangers won the home leg 3-2 and followed up with another three in Portugal. The home side's four goals were to no avail and the referee Mr. Van Ravens also had an unhappy night after mistakenly ordering a penalty shoot-out. He was later suspended for his blunder. Rangers didn't blunder in the quarter-final when they beat Torino 2-1, on aggregate, to set up another two meetings with Bayern Munich.

Following a splendid 1-1 draw in Munich, goals from Sandy Jardine and Derek Parlane, without reply, gave the Gers sweet revenge at Ibrox. There were more wild celebrations the following month when two goals by Johnston and another by Stein proved just enough to hold off Moscow Dynamo 3-2 in the final. The relief and joy was immeasurable as John Greig collected the trophy: Rangers had been bridesmaids in this competition on two previous occasions (in 1960-

John Greig and Sandy Jardine, long-serving Rangers players who had an important role in the 1971-72 European Cup Winners' Cup winning team.

61 and 1966-67). Although the unruly pitch invasions by some over-enthusiastic fans stole the headlines, nothing could deprive Rangers of the credit for their European performances in 1971-72.

Sadly, the 'Battle of Barcelona' did deprive Rangers of the opportunity of defending their trophy when they collected a one year ban from European competitions.

Jock Wallace stepped up from coach to become manager in the summer of 1972. His side handicapped themselves in the League in 1972-73 by losing 3 out of their first 5 fixtures. However, a superb run of 16 consecutive victories between late December and early April gave the club a squeak at the title. Although the Gers led the table for most of the post Christmas period, Celtic had an extra game up their sleeves and went past their great rivals to take the Championship by one point. Rangers' top scorer was Parlane with 19.

Parlane was on target in the Scottish Cup final as the Gers inflicted a degree of revenge by beating Celtic 3-2. Alfie Conn and Tom Forsyth were the other scorers. Earlier in 1972-73 a single Hibs goal punctured Rangers' League Cup ambitions in a Hampden Park semi-final.

European Cup Winners' Cup football returned to Ibrox in 1973-74; but, after by-passing Ankaragucu, Rangers found Borussia Moenchengladbach too strong for them in the second round. They reached the semi-final stage of the League Cup but were defeated 3-1 by Celtic; while hopes of retaining the Scottish Cup evaporated in the fourth round when Dundee netted three second half goals without reply at Ibrox.

Another sluggish start, when they lost 3 of their first 4 home games (against Celtic, Hearts and East Fife), virtually wrecked the Gers' bid to block Celtic taking a ninth successive title. Wallace's side won 7 of their last 9 fixtures, but had to be satisfied with third place, with Hibs sandwiched between the two great Glasgow rivals as the 1973-74 runners-up.

Rangers finally broke Celtic's stranglehold on the title twelve months later when they finished 7 points clear of Hibs, with the previous Champions a further 4 points back in third. Rangers fully deserved their first title in 11 seasons. They defeated Celtic in both League games and were not headed after winning the Old Firm home fixture 3-0 in early January.

Of the 19 players Jock Wallace called upon, only goalkeeper Stuart Kennedy and Jardine, the 'Player of the Year', were ever-presents. For the third successive season, Parlane (with 17) was the top scorer.

Rangers did not win a knock-out Cup tie in 1974-75, but made up for it the following term when they won both domestic cup competitions and gloriously completed a clean sweep by taking the first ever Premier Division title. The Gers won 3 of the 5 Old Firm battles 1-0, the other two ending in draws.

Alex MacDonald netted the goal that defeated Celtic 1-0 as Rangers secured the League Cup at Hampden Park towards the end of October. MacDonald was also on target in the Scottish Cup final when Hearts were thumped 3-1. Johnstone scored a brace in that game and was also the club's leading League scorer (with 15). The Ibrox club finished 6 points ahead of second placed Celtic and had ever-present skipper John Greig named by the Scottish Football Writers' Association as the 'Player of the Year' for an unprecedented second time.

Jock Wallace surprised many observers in the second half of the season when he refused to disrupt a settled team and left Jardine and Parlane on the bench for several games after they had recovered from injury. The main beneficiary of Parlane's absence was young Martin Henderson, who finished second top scorer with 10 goals.

The only down note of 1975-76 was the club's exit from the European Cup at the second round stage. After disposing of Bohemians, the Gers found St. Etienne too hot to handle and lost both legs.

The following term's European Cup campaign was even shorter as they crashed out at the first hurdle to FC Zurich, 2-1 on aggregate. And twelve months after taking all the domestic honours Rangers ended up completely empty-handed. Aberdeen crushed them 5-1 in a League Cup semi-final; while a single penalty gave the green and white half of Glasgow a Scottish Cup final victory the following May.

Meanwhile the League Championship trophy had also gone to Celtic Park. The Gers handicapped themselves by only winning 2 of their first 8 games and were always playing catch-up in 1976-77. They had no chance of pegging back Celtic (who finished 9 points clear) but at least managed to bull-doze their way into second place.

Defeats in the first two League games did not bode well for 1977-78; but in fact this was to be another season of treble honours. Rangers leapt from bottom of the early tables to the top (after beating Aberdeen) in October. The Dons became their only serious challengers for the crown and Rangers were pushed all the way to the line. The Gers lost only 3 more times after those opening two defeats; but still could not afford any lapses in the run-in. They won their last four matches to stay two points ahead at the finish.

'Player of the Year' Johnstone was the Division's top scorer with 25 goals,

The Rangers and Celtic Captains, John Greig and Kenny Dalglish, shake hands before another hard fought Old Firm derby in 1977.

while Gordon Smith bagged 20. Smith, Davie Cooper and Bobby Russell were the new blood that made such a big difference in 1977-78. The only blot on the copy-book was in the European Cup Winners' Cup. The Gers squeaked past Young Boys in the Preliminary round but crashed out in Holland against Twente.

However, Rangers went on to win both domestic cup finals by a 2-1 margin. Aberdeen were defeated in the Scottish Cup final, with Alex MacDonald and Johnstone on the score-sheet. Nearly two months earlier the scorers were Cooper and Smith in the extra-time victory over Celtic in the League Cup final. Rangers had been given a nasty scare in the semi-final by Forfar Athletic. The Second Division side were only 7 minutes from victory; but Wallace's men drew level and then then broke the Loons' hearts by winning 5-2 in extra-time.

After his side had secured their second treble in three seasons, Jock Wallace left to become manager of Leicester City. His old skipper John Greig moved into the managerial office.

Greig's first season was not totally satisfactory because the League title was lost to Celtic. However, both domestic cups were retained and Rangers enjoyed two excellent victories in the European Cup before exiting at the hands of Cologne in the quarter-finals.

Juventus were their first European opponents. A 1-0 first leg deficit was overturned as the Gers progressed with goals by Alex MacDonald and Smith at Ibrox. Greig's side used the reverse route to get round PSV Eindhoven in the second round. After a goalless stalemate at Ibrox, Rangers came from behind to win 3-2 in Holland.

After beating Celtic in extra-time in the semi-final, Rangers won the League Cup by beating Aberdeen 2-1 at Hampden Park. The Scottish Cup final with Hibs went to three games (including two lots of extra-time); the first two provided little excitement and no goals, but the second replay was much more interesting with five goals. Two by Johnstone and an own-goal was just enough to nudge the trophy back to Ibrox. Sadly there was only a sparse crowd of 30,602 to enjoy the entertainment.

An abysmal start of only one win from the first 9 games meant Rangers had to work hard to move into contention with the League leaders. Nevertheless a run of excellent results took them to the top of the table in February. However, they could not quite sustain their challenge and after losing two of their last three (including the crucial final away Old Firm fixture) they handed the trophy to Celtic by 2 points. The Gers had let silly points slip all through 1978-79 with 8 different sides (all but Morton) claiming League successes over them.

The following season was very disappointing for Rangers. They exited the Bell's League Cup in the third round at Aberdeen. Then they threw away any chance of winning the 1979-80 title by winning only 3 games out of ten in early Winter. They eventually finished 5th, 11 points adrift of the Champions Aberdeen.

After beating Lilleström and Fortuna Dusseldorf, their dreams of further Cup Winners' Cup glory were punctured by Valencia who won 3-1 at Ibrox, after the first leg in Spain had finished so promisingly at 1-1. Rangers' last hope of silverware (and qualification for Europe) rested with the Scottish Cup, but they were beaten by a single goal in extra-time of an Old Firm final.

The Gers were back at Hampden Park to contest the Scottish Cup final twelve months later. They needed a replay but eventually triumphed over Dundee United 4-1 with goals from Cooper, Russell and John MacDonald (2). That victory was the highlight of their season, after again exiting to Aberdeen in the Bell's League Cup and once more dropping out of League contention before Winter set in (winning only 3 out of 13 fixtures between early October and mid-January). They eventually finished 1980-81 in third, 12 points behind the

Champions Celtic.

Greig's side finished in the same position and with the same number of points behind the same Champions in 1981-82. They could not quite get on terms after making a mediocre start.

Dukla Prague knocked them out of the European Cup Winners' Cup at the first hurdle; while Aberdeen defeated them 4-1 in the Scottish Cup final. However, the Gers did take one piece of silverware in 1981-82 in the form of the Scottish League Cup by beating Dundee United 2-1 in the final.

Twelve months later, Rangers were on the wrong end of the same scoreline as Celtic won the League Cup final. After they had defeated Borussia Dortmund, the Gers' 1982-83 UEFA Cup run was brought to a juddering end (6-2 on aggregate) by another German side, Cologne.

Rangers were singularly average in the League. They never headed the table and remained stuck in 4th place from the last day in October to the end of the season. There was more agony for the Gers in the final of the Scottish Cup when Aberdeen pipped them again - this time by a single goal. There was a small consolation in that by reaching the final, the Gers qualified again for Europe because Aberdeen later lifted the European Cup Winners' Cup.

Ironically the same club, Porto, knocked both Scottish sides out of the 1983-84 Cup Winners' Cup competition. Rangers exited on away goals in the second round; but at least ran off some steam beforehand when they thumped Valetta 18-0 on aggregate.

Only 3 of the first 12 games were won in 1983-84, and by the time Rangers recovered John Greig had been replaced by his former boss Jock Wallace. The Gers lost only one of the last 24 fixtures but still finished as low as 4th, 15 points behind the Champions Aberdeen.

Dundee proved to be too good for them in the Scottish Cup; but Wallace's side did collect the League Cup by winning an Old Firm final 3-2 with Ally McCoist netting a hat-trick.

A poor spell of just 2 wins in 11 games, in the new year, scuppered any chance of League success in 1984-85 and the Gers finished in 4th yet again; behind Aberdeen, Celtic and Dundee United.

Their progress in the Scottish Cup was again halted by Dundee; but the League (now Skol) Cup was retained with a 1-0 final victory over Dundee United.

The Gers did not have much joy in the 1984-85 UEFA Cup. After just seeing off Bohemians 4-3 in the first round, they slipped out by the same aggregate score-line to Internazionale.

Twelve months later their UEFA Cup exit came in the first round at the hands of Atletico Osasuna. Rangers had little cup luck domestically either; failing in the third round of the Scottish Cup and losing to Hibs, after 3 games, in a Skol Cup semi-final.

There was early promise in the League, with 5 wins from the first 6 matches, but a lack of consistency, especially on their travels (where they lost 10 times), pushed the Gers down to 5th. Ally McCoist finished as the Division's top scorer in 1985-86, with 24 goals.

Jock Wallace vacated the Ibrox manager's chair for the second time and was replaced by Graeme Souness in May 1986. The new player-manager made the worst possible start when he was dismissed after a flare-up in the opening day defeat by Hibs in his home city of Edinburgh. However, Souness' first trophy as a manager was not too far away as his side beat Celtic 2-1 in an October Skol Cup final.

There was no joy in the other two cups in 1986-87. Borussia Moenchengladbach ended their hopes in the UEFA Cup third round after Ilves and Boavista had been side-stepped in the early proceedings. More surprisingly, Premier

Derek Johnstone who was a faithful servant of Rangers for many years before leaving to become Manager of Partick Thistle in July 1986.

Division strugglers Hamilton ended their interest in the Scottish Cup at the first hurdle.

However, that Ibrox defeat was soon forgotten as the League race hotted up and Rangers gobbled up Celtic's big lead. In the end Souness' expensively assembled side finished 9 points clear after winning 20 of their last 25 fixtures. McCoist's 33 goals made him the top scorer, while Robert Fleck netted a handy 20. It was the club's first title in nine years and was ample proof that the money had been soundly spent. Chris Woods had a fine season between the posts and fellow England international Terry Butcher, the team captain, added solidity to the defence.

It was a different story in 1987-88 when they never really recovered from a poor start of just one win from 5 games. Nevertheless, 15 victories from the next 20 fixtures put them into contention but they could not quite carry their challenge through and finished in third place, 12 points adrift of the Champions Celtic. The loss of Butcher with a broken leg was a disruptive factor and, in addition, not all the numerous new purchases paid-off. Among the new signings were the English contingent of Mark Falco, Graham Roberts, Trevor Francis, Ray Wilkins and Mark Walters.

Dunfermline edged them out of the Scottish Cup, but Rangers retained the Skol Cup by defeating Aberdeen on penalties after a 3-3 deadlock. The Gers' 1987-88 European Cup run involved games with 3 Eastern European sides. After disposing of Dynamo Kiev and Gornik Zabre, they came unstuck against Steaua Bucharest.

There were only two European trips the following term, in the UEFA Cup, to GKS Katowice and then, unsuccessfully, to Cologne. However, Rangers gorged themselves domestically and only a single Celtic goal in the Scottish Cup final deprived them of another treble.

Souness' side never relinquished League leadership after hitting the front at the end of August and lost only six fixtures in 1988-89. Gary Stevens added further stability to the defence, while yet another English recruit, Kevin Drinkell, top scored (with 12). Richard Gough had an excellent season and collected the 'Player of the Year' award.

The Skol Cup was retained for the third successive term, two goals from McCoist and one from Ian Ferguson being just enough to defeat Aberdeen.

Twelve months later, Aberdeen exacted revenge in the final of the same tournament with a 2-1 victory after extra-time. Early exits at the hands of Bayern Munich and Celtic in the European Cup and Scottish Cup, respectively, allowed

Rangers to concentrate on retaining the Premier Division title.

After a shaky start of just one success in six, the Gers picked up ground and hit the front with 14 wins in 17 games. They finished 1989-90 seven points ahead of Aberdeen, Mo Johnston top scoring with 15.

The lure of the top Anfield job was too great for Graeme Souness to ignore and, after securing three titles and three Skol Cups in four seasons, he was succeeded by his assistant Walter Smith. Souness had gone but it was very much business as usual with the 1990-91 Skol Cup and Scottish League titles heading to Ibrox.

Walters and Gough netted to give the Gers a 2-1 edge after extra-time in an Old Firm Skol Cup. However, Celtic got some revenge later in the term when they scuppered Rangers' Scottish Cup hopes.

A very close League race came down to a last day shoot-out with Aberdeen. Rangers had seemed sure to win the title in mid-season, but the Dons had kept plugging away and the final margin was two Mark Hateley goals on the last day and two points over the campaign. Hateley (with 10) was one of 4 players to hit double figures. Walters top scored with 12, in front of Johnston and McCoist (on 11 apiece).

In the 1990-91 European Cup, Rangers enjoyed themselves again against Valetta, netting 10 times over the 180 minutes; but as usual, they ran out of ammo when it really mattered against Red Star Belgrade.

Smith's side hit the buffers in the first round of the following season's European Cup when they lost to Sparta Prague on away goals. Hopes of a sixth successive Skol Cup final appearance were ended by Hibs at the semi-final stage. Conversely, the Gers won the Scottish Cup for the first time in 11 seasons when McCoist and Hateley were on the mark in a 2-1 success over Airdrieonians.

McCoist was the 1991-92 'Player of the Year' and the League's top scorer. He netted 34 times and together with Hateley shared 55 of the 101 goals that put Rangers on course for their fourth successive title. Thirty (out of 44) games were won including 19 away, where they dropped just 5 points. Hearts and Celtic still gave them a fight, but the final points margins were 9 and 10, respectively.

It was a similar story in the League in 1992-93, as they notched up 33 victories and had 9 points to spare over Aberdeen. McCoist was the League's top scorer again, with another 34, and Hateley 19 as Rangers netted another 97 goals. Goalkeeper Andy Goram collected the 'Player of the Year' award.

Aberdeen finished as bridesmaids twice more that season as Smith's side registered the treble. The Dons were defeated 2-1 in both cup finals. Stuart

McCall gave Rangers the lead in the Skol Cup, but it needed an extra-time own-goal to send the trophy to Ibrox. Neil Murray and Hateley were on the score-sheet in the Scottish Cup triumph as the Gers' fans celebrated their third treble in 16 campaigns.

Victories home and away over Lyngby and Leeds United (the latter two by 2-1 in the 'Battles of Britain') set the Gers up for six games in the European Champions League in 1992-93. Rangers drew twice with Marseille; and collected 3 points out of 4 from encounters with CSKA Moscow and FC Brugge; yet failed to reach the final after finishing one point behind the French side in the Group table.

Rangers won only 3 of the first 10 League fixtures in 1993-94, but still came good and won the title again, despite easing up and taking just 2 points from their last 5 games. The final margin was 3 points (over Aberdeen) with Hateley's 22 goals making him the Division's top scorer. The tall striker was also voted 'Player of the Year', the first Englishman to receive the award from the Scottish Football Writers' Association.

Both domestic cup finals were reached with mixed results. Hibernian were beaten 2-1 at Celtic Park in the Skol Cup; but the Gers lost to a single second half Dundee United goal in the Scottish Cup.

Rangers missed the chance of participating in the lucrative part of the 1993-94 European Cup when they exited on away goals to Levski Sofia in the first round.

Twelve months later the Gers suffered more European Cup agony when they crashed out in the Preliminary round to AEK Athens. Rangers also made little impression in the domestic cups. Falkirk knocked them out of the last 16 of the Coca-Cola Cup and Hearts stopped them at the same stage of the Scottish Cup.

While Smith's side were never quite at their best during 1994-95, they still romped to their seventh successive title, 15 points clear of Motherwell. The star player was undoubtedly Brian Laudrup and he was a popular choice as 'Player of the Year'.

1970-71

1	Aug	29	(a)	St. Mirren	D	0-0		27,400
2	Sep	5	(h)	Falkirk	W	2-0	Johnston 2 (1 pen)	32,000
3		12	(a)	Celtic	L	0-2		73,000
4		19	(h)	Cowdenbeath	W	5-0	Jackson, Greig 2, Johnston 2	30,000
5		26	(a)	Dundee U	W	2-0	Conn, Fyfe	23,000
6	Oct	3	(h)	Motherwell	W	3-1	McDonald, Stein, Johnston	25,000
7		10	(a)	Hearts	W	1-0	Johnston (pen)	32,500
8		17	(h)	Aberdeen	L	0-2		32,000
9		31	(h)	Airdrieonians	W	5-0	Johnston 2 (1 pen), Stein 2, Conn	28,788
10	Nov	7	(a)	Dunfermline Ath	D	1-1	Jackson	17,000
11		14	(h)	Clyde	W	5-0	Stein 2, Johnston (pen), Johnstone, Mulherron (og)	25,000
12		21	(a)	Ayr U	L	1-2	Young (og)	20,000
13		25	(a)	Hibernian	L	2-3	Johnstone, Stein	18,032
14		28	(a)	Morton	W	2-1	Conn, Fyfe	15,000
15	Dec	5	(h)	Dundee	D	0-0		30,000
16		12	(a)	St. Johnstone	L	1-2	Fyfe	10,500
17		19	(h)	Kilmarnock	W	4-2	Jackson, McDonald, Johnstone 2	22,000
18		26	(h)	St. Mirren	W	1-0	Greig	20,000
19	Jan	1	(a)	Falkirk	L	1-3	Conn	18,000
20		2	(h)	Celtic	D	1-1	Johnston	80,000
21		16	(h)	Dundee U	D	1-1	Greig	27,500
22		30	(a)	Motherwell	W	2-1	Mathieson, Stein	17,500
23	Feb	6	(h)	Hearts	W	1-0	Henderson	18,000
24		20	(a)	Aberdeen	D	0-0		36,000
25		27	(h)	Hibernian	D	1-1	Greig	22,000
26	Mar	10	(a)	Airdrieonians	L	3-4	McDonald A 2, Stein	7,000
27		13	(h)	Dunfermline Ath	W	2-0	Henderson, Greig	21,580
28		20	(a)	Clyde	D	2-2	Johnston, Stein	10,500
29		27	(h)	Ayr U	W	2-0	Greig, Johnston	20,000
30	Apr	3	(h)	Morton	D	0-0		14,000
31		10	(a)	Dundee	L	0-1		13,000
32		14	(a)	Cowdenbeath	W	3-1	Jardine, Greig, Stein	5,000
33		17	(h)	St. Johnstone	L	0-2		17,566
34		24	(a)	Kilmarnock	W	4-1	Henderson, Miller, Stein, McDonald	9,500

FINAL LEAGUE POSITION : 4th in Division One

Appearances

Sub. Appearances

Goals

McCloy	Jardine	Miller	Greig	McKinnon	Jackson	Fyfe	Conn	Stein	McDonald A	Johnston	Penman	Henderson	Johnstone	Smith	McCallum	Parlane	Semple	Neef	Mathieson	McDonald J	Watson	No.
1	2	3	4	5	6	7	8	9	10	11												1
1	2	3	4	5	6	7	8	9	10	11												2
1	2	3	4	5	6	7*	11	9	8	10	12											3
1	2	3	4	5	6	11	8		10	9		7										4
1	2	3	4	5	6	7	8	9	10	11												5
1	2	3		5	6	8	4	9*	10	11		7	12									6
1	2	3	4	5	6	12	8*	9	10	11		7										7
1	2	3	4	5	6	8		9	10	11		7		12								8
1	2	3		5	6		4	10	8	11		7	9									9
1	2	3	4*	5	6		8	10	12	11		7	9									10
1	2	3		5	6	12	4*	10	8	11		7	9									11
1	2	3		5	6	10	4*	9	8	11		7	12									12
1	2	3		5	6	11	4	10	8			7*	9	12								13
1	2	3		5	6	12	4	10	8	11		7	9*									14
1	2	3	4	5	6	10	8	9		11		7										15
1	2	3	4	5	6	11*		9	8			7	12	10								16
1	2	3	4	5	6		8	11				7	9	10								17
1	2	3			6	7	4		10				9		5	8	11					18
	2		4	5	6		8	11	12			7*	9	10				1	3			19
	2		4	5	6		8	11	12			7*	9	10				1	3			20
	2		4	5	6		8	9	12	11		7		10				1	3*			21
1	2		4	5	6		8*	9	12	11		7		10					3			22
1	2		4	5	6		12	8		11		7	9*	10					3			23
1	2		4	5	6		8	9	10	11*		7	12						3			24
1	2		4	5			9	8				7		10		12			3	11*	6	25
1	2		4	5	6		9	8		11		7		10*		12			3			26
1	2		4	5	6		9	8	10			7							3	11		27
1	2		4	5	6		10	9	8*	11	12	7							3			28
1	2	3	4	5	6		12	10	8			7					9			11*		29
1	2		4	5	6	12	9	11	8*			7		10					3			30
1	4*		10	5	6		9	8		11	12	7							3		2	31
1			4	5	6		9	8		11	12	7		10					3		2	32
1		2	4	5	6		9	10	11	8		7							3			33
1	2	3		5	6	4	10	8		11		7	9									34
31	32	22	26	32	34	11	23	30	27	26	3	29	12	9	1	2	2	3	14	3	3	
						3	2		6		4		4	2		2						
	1	1	8		3	3	4	11	5	11		3	5						1			

1971-72

#	Month	Date		Opponent	Res	Score	Scorers	Attendance
1	Sep	4	(a)	Partick T	L	2-3	MacDonald A, Stein	22,000
2		11	(h)	Celtic	L	2-3	Johnston W (pen), Stein	69,000
3		18	(a)	Falkirk	W	3-0	Greig 2, Stein	20,000
4		25	(h)	Aberdeen	L	0-2		38,000
5	Oct	2	(a)	Hearts	L	1-2	Johnston W	28,000
6		9	(h)	East Fife	W	3-0	Jardine (pen), Fyfe, MacDonald A	20,000
7		16	(a)	Dundee U	W	5-1	Jardine, Greig, MacDonald A 2, Stein	17,000
8		23	(h)	Motherwell	W	4-0	Jardine, Fyfe 2, MacDonald A	20,000
9		30	(h)	Kilmarnock	W	3-1	MacDonald A 2, Stein	22,000
10	Nov	6	(a)	St. Johnstone	W	4-1	Johnston W 3 (3 pens), MacDonald A	20,000
11		13	(h)	Dundee	L	2-3	Johnston W 2	35,000
12		20	(a)	Morton	W	2-1	Greig, Johnston W	12,000
13		27	(a)	Ayr U	W	2-1	Henderson, Stein	15,100
14	Dec	4	(h)	Clyde	W	1-0	Stein	22,000
15		11	(a)	Dunfermline Ath	W	2-0	Greig, Johnston W	14,000
16		18	(h)	Airdrieonians	W	3-0	Jardine (pen), Fyfe, Stein	18,000
17		25	(a)	Hibernian	W	1-0	Stein	30,000
18	Jan	1	(h)	Partick T	W	2-1	Greig, Johnstone D	40,000
19		3	(a)	Celtic	L	1-2	Stein	77,811
20		8	(h)	Falkirk	W	3-1	Greig, Jackson, MacDonald I	20,000
21		15	(a)	Aberdeen	D	0-0		36,000
22		22	(h)	Hearts	W	6-0	Greig, Conn, Johnston W, Johnstone D 3	35,000
23		29	(a)	East Fife	W	1-0	Johnstone D	12,018
24	Feb	12	(h)	Dundee U	W	1-0	Smith	15,000
25		19	(a)	Motherwell	L	0-2		16,192
26	Mar	4	(a)	Kilmarnock	W	2-1	Jardine, Conn	18,000
27		11	(h)	St. Johnstone	W	2-0	Johnstone D, McLean	25,000
28		25	(h)	Morton	L	1-2	Jackson	16,000
29	Apr	8	(a)	Clyde	D	1-1	Johnston W	7,500
30		10	(a)	Dundee	L	0-2		12,000
31		22	(a)	Airdrieonians	W	3-0	Fyfe, Penman 2	10,000
32		27	(h)	Dunfermline Ath	L	3-4	MacDonald A 2, Stein	3,000
33		29	(h)	Hibernian	L	1-2	Johnstone D	11,000
34	May	1	(h)	Ayr U	W	4-2	Conn, Fyfe, MacDonald A, Penman	3,000

FINAL LEAGUE POSITION : 3rd in Division One

Appearances

Sub. Appearances

Goals

McCloy	Jardine	Mathieson	Greig	McKinnon	MacDonald A	McLean	Penman	Stein	Denny	Johnston W	Conn	Jackson	Smith	Fyfe	Henderson	Johnstone D	McDonald I	Miller	Parlane	Match
1	2	3	4	5	6	7	8	9	10*	11	12									1
1	2	3	4		6	7*	8	9		11	10	5			12					2
1	2	3	4	5	10		7	9		11	8	6								3
1	2	3	4		10*	12	7	9		11	8	5	6							4
1	2	3	4	5	10	8*	12	9		11		6			7					5
1	4	3	2	5	11			9			8		6	10	7					6
1	4	3	2	5	11		8	9					6	10	7					7
1	4	3	2	5	11			9			8		6	10	7					8
1	4	3	2	5	11		8	9					6	10	7					9
1	4	3	2		11			9			12	8	5	6	10*	7				10
1	4	3	2		11			9			10	8	5	6		7				11
1	2	3	4		10	7*		9		11	12	5	6	8						12
1	2	3	4		10			9		11	8		6		7	5				13
1	4	3			10			9	2	11			6	8	7	5				14
1	2	3	4		10	8		9		11*			6	12	7	5				15
1	2	3*	4		11	7		9			8	5	6	10	12					16
1	2		4		10	7		9	3	11	8	5	6							17
1	2		4		10	7		9	3		8	5	6			12	11*			18
1	2	3	4		10	7		9		11		5	6			8				19
1	2	3	4		10	7		9			8	5	6				11			20
1	2	3	4		10	7		9*			8	12	6			5	11			21
1	2	3	4		10	7				11	8	5	6			9				22
1	2	3	4		10	7				11	8	5	6			9				23
1	2	3	4		10	7			12		8	5	6			9	11*			24
1	2		4		12	7		9			8	5	6			10	11*	3		25
1	2	3	4		11	7		9		10	8	5	6							26
1		3	4			7			2	10	8	5	6	12		9	11*			27
1		3			10		7*	9	2		4	5	6	12		8	11			28
1	2	3	4			7				11	10*	5	6	12	9			8		29
1	2	3	4		11	8		9				5	6	7				10		30
1					11		8		2		4	5	6	9	7	10			3	31
1	2	3			11			9		10	4	5	6		7	8				32
1	2	3			4		8	7	12	10		5*	6		11	9				33
1	2	3			10	7*	8	9		11	4		6	12	5					34
34	31	30	28	7	31	21	10	28	7	23	21	24	30	9	13	16	7	2	2	
						1	1	1			2	1	2	1		5	2			
	5		8		11	1	3	11		11	3	2	1		6	1	7		1	

1972-73

1	Sep	2	(a)	Ayr U	L	1-2	Johnston	14,500
2		9	(h)	Partick T	W	2-1	Johnston, MacDonald	28,000
3		16	(a)	Celtic	L	1-3	Greig	50,416
4		23	(h)	Falkirk	W	1-0	McLean (pen)	12,000
5		30	(a)	Kilmarnock	L	1-2	McLean	14,000
6	Oct	7	(h)	Morton	D	1-1	Fyfe	15,000
7		14	(a)	Motherwell	W	2-0	Parlane (pen), Young	17,621
8		21	(a)	Arbroath	W	2-1	Parlane, Mason	8,400
9		28	(h)	St. Johnstone	W	5-1	Conn 2, Parlane 2, Johnston	20,000
10	Nov	4	(a)	Dundee	D	1-1	Conn	19,600
11		11	(h)	Airdrieonians	W	1-0	Conn	17,000
12		18	(a)	Hibernian	W	2-1	Conn, Fyfe	33,356
13		25	(h)	Dumbarton	W	3-1	Conn, Parlane, Young	14,500
14	Dec	2	(h)	Hearts	L	0-1		22,000
15		9	(a)	Dundee U	W	4-1	Jardine, Conn, Parlane 2	11,000
16		16	(h)	Aberdeen	D	0-0		30,000
17		23	(a)	East Fife	W	4-0	Parlane, Johnstone 2, Young	8,608
18		30	(h)	Ayr U	W	2-1	Conn, Parlane	17,653
19	Jan	1	(a)	Partick T	W	1-0	Young	18,500
20		6	(h)	Celtic	W	2-1	Conn, Parlane	67,000
21		13	(a)	Falkirk	W	4-2	Conn, Parlane (pen), Young 2	17,000
22		20	(h)	Kilmarnock	W	4-0	Greig, Parlane 2, Young	14,000
23		27	(a)	Morton	W	2-1	MacDonald, Young	14,000
24	Feb	10	(h)	Motherwell	W	2-1	Jardine, Young	22,000
25		19	(h)	Arbroath	W	5-0	Greig, Parlane 2, Young, Miller	12,000
26	Mar	3	(a)	St. Johnstone	W	2-1	Mason, Miller	12,000
27		10	(h)	Dundee	W	3-1	MacDonald, Parlane 2	30,000
28		20	(a)	Airdrieonians	W	6-2	Greig, McLean, Parlane, Johnstone, Young, Mason	18,000
29		24	(h)	Hibernian	W	1-0	McLean	51,200
30		31	(a)	Dumbarton	W	2-1	Parlane, Young	13,000
31	Apr	7	(a)	Hearts	W	1-0	Greig	24,000
32		14	(h)	Dundee U	W	2-1	Greig 2	30,000
33		21	(a)	Aberdeen	D	2-2	McLean, Conn	32,000
34		28	(h)	East Fife	W	2-0	Conn, Young	27,544

FINAL LEAGUE POSITION : 2nd in Division One

Appearances

Sub. Appearances

Goals

McCloy	Jardine	Mathieson	Greig	Jackson	Johnstone	McLean	Denny	Johnston	Stein	Fyfe	MacDonald	Smith	Conn	Parlane	Donaldson	Young	Forsyth	Mason	Neef	Miller	No.
1	2	3	4	5	6	7	8	9	10	11*	12										1
1	2	3	4	5	9	7	8	11			10	6									2
1	2	3	4	5	9		8	11*	7		10	6	12								3
1	2	3	4	5	9	7		11			10	6		8							4
1	2	3	4	5	9	7			12		11	6	10*	8							5
1	8	3	4	5	9		2			7	10		12	6*	11						6
1	2	3	4		5							6	7	9		11	8	10			7
	2	3	4		5							6	7	9		11	8	10	1		8
1	2	3	4		5							6	7*	9	12	11	8	10			9
1	2	3	4		5							6	7	9	8	11		10			10
1	2	3	4*		5					12	11	6	7	9	8			10			11
1	2	3	4		5				8		11	6	7	9				10			12
1	2	3	4		5					12	8	6	7	9		11		10*			13
1	2	3	4		5					12	8	6	7	9		11		10*			14
1	2	3			5	7					4	6	8	9		11		10			15
1	2	3			5	7				12	4	6	8*	9		11		10			16
1	2	3	10		5	7					4		9			11	6	8			17
1	2	3	4	5	12							6	7	9		11	8	10*			18
1	2	3	4		5	7					10	6		9		11	8				19
1	2	3	4		5						10	6	7	9		11	8				20
1	2	3	4			7					10	6	8	9		11	5				21
1	2	3	4		5	7					10	6*		9	12	11	8				22
1	2	3	4		5	7				12	10	6		9*		11	8				23
1	2	3	4			7	8				10	6		9		11	5				24
1	2	3	4		5	7						6		9*		11	8	12		10	25
1	2	3			5	7					4	6		9		11	8	12		10*	26
1	4	3			5	7	2*				10	6		9		11	8	12			27
1	2	3	4		5	7					10	6		9*		11	8	12			28
1	2	3	4		5	7					10	6		9		11	8				29
1	2	3	4		5	7					10	6*		9		11	8	12			30
1	2	3	4		5	7					10	6*	12	9		11	8				31
1	2	3	4		5	7						6	10	9		11	8				32
1	2	3	4		5	7					10	6	11	9			8				33
1	2	3	4		5	7						6	10	9		11	8				34
33	34	34	30	7	31	22	6	4	2	3	27	29	18	29	3	26	21	12	1	2	
			2				1			3	2		2	1	2			4		1	
	2		7	4	5	2					2	3	12	19		13	3	2			

1973-74

1	Sep	1	(h)	Ayr U	D	0-0		30,000
2		8	(a)	Partick T	W	1-0	Scott	21,000
3		15	(h)	Celtic	L	0-1		60,000
4		29	(h)	Hearts	L	0-3		30,000
5	Oct	6	(a)	Arbroath	W	2-1	O'Hara 2	7,170
6		13	(h)	East Fife	L	0-1		20,000
7		20	(a)	Dundee U	W	3-1	Conn 2, O'Hara	10,000
8		27	(h)	Hibernian	W	4-0	Jardine 2 (2 pens), Greig, Conn	30,000
9	Nov	3	(a)	Dunfermline A	D	2-2	O'Hara, Jackson	17,000
10		10	(h)	Morton	W	1-0	Greig	15,000
11		17	(h)	Falkirk	W	2-1	Greig 2	15,000
12		24	(a)	Clyde	W	2-0	MacDonald, Jackson	12,000
13	Dec	15	(h)	St. Johnstone	W	5-1	MacDonald, Smith, Parlane, Conn, Young	6,000
14		22	(a)	Dumbarton	W	2-0	Parlane, Young	7,000
15		29	(a)	Ayr U	W	1-0	Parlane	17,000
16	Jan	1	(h)	Partick T	D	1-1	Parlane (pen)	16,000
17		5	(a)	Celtic	L	0-1		55,000
18		12	(h)	Aberdeen	D	1-1	McLean	16,000
19		19	(a)	Hearts	W	4-2	Parlane 4 (1 pen)	20,000
20	Feb	2	(h)	Arbroath	L	2-3	McLean, Parlane (pen)	15,000
21		9	(a)	East Fife	W	3-0	McLean, Scott, Hamilton	8,499
22		24	(h)	Dundee U	W	3-1	Parlane 2 (1 pen), Young	15,500
23	Mar	2	(a)	Hibernian	L	1-3	McLean	23,149
24		16	(a)	Morton	W	3-2	Parlane (pen), Jackson 2	9,000
25		23	(a)	Falkirk	D	0-0		10,000
26		30	(h)	Clyde	W	4-0	Greig, Johnstone, MacDonald, Scott	10,000
27	Apr	2	(h)	Dunfermline A	W	3-0	Parlane (pen), Scott, Fyfe	7,000
28		6	(a)	Motherwell	W	4-1	Scott, Young 2, Fyfe	13,346
29		13	(h)	Dundee	L	1-2	Jardine (pen)	25,000
30		17	(a)	Aberdeen	D	1-1	Greig	18,000
31		20	(a)	St. Johnstone	W	3-1	Young, Fyfe 2	7,500
32		24	(h)	Motherwell	W	2-1	Parlane, Scott	10,000
33		27	(h)	Dumbarton	W	3-1	Scott 2, Fyfe	10,000
34		29	(a)	Dundee	W	3-2	Young, Fyfe 2	10,578

FINAL LEAGUE POSITION : 3rd in Division One

Appearances

Sub. Appearances

Goals

McCloy	Jardine	Mathieson	Greig	Johnstone	MacDonald	McLean	Forsyth	O'Hara	Parlane	Smith	Conn	Denny	Scott	Young	Houston	Kennedy	Morris	Jackson	Fyfe	Hamilton	McDougall	Hunter	#
1	2	3	4	5	6	7	8	9*	10	11†	12	13											1
1	2	3	4*	5	6	7	8	9	13	12	11†		10										2
1	2	3	4	5	6	7*	8		9		10		12	11									3
1	2	3	4	5	6	7*	8		9		10		12	11†	13								4
1	2	3	4	5	6	7	8	9			12		10*	11									5
	2	3	4	5	6	7	8		10				9*	11		1		12					6
1	2	3	4	5	6	7	8	9		13	12		10*	11†									7
1	2	3	4	5	6	7	8	9			10			11									8
1	2	3	4		6	7	8	12	9*		10			11				5					9
1	2	3	4		6	7	8	9			10*			11				5	12				10
1	2	3	4	10	11	7	8	9							6			5					11
1	2	3	4		10	7	8	9					11		6			5					12
1	2	3	4	5	11	12	8		9	6	10*		7										13
1	2	3	4	5	11		8	10	9*	6			12	7									14
1	2	3	4	5	11		8	10	9	6				7									15
1	2	3	4	5	12		8	10	9	6			11*	7									16
1	2	3	4	5	10		8		9				11*	7	6				12				17
1	2	3	4	5	10	7	6	8	9					11*					12				18
1	2	3	4*	5		7	8	9		6			10				11		12				19
	2	3	5			7	4	9		6			8*	13			11†		12	10		1	20
	2	3	6			7	4	9					8				11	5		10		1	21
	2	3	12	6		7	4	9					10*	11				5		8		1	22
1	2	3	12		6	10	7	4	9*				8	11				5					23
1	2	3	8		6	10	7	4	9					11				5					24
1	2	3	4		6	10	7	8	9					11				5					25
1	2	3	4*	5	10				9				8	7			11†	6	13		12		26
1	2		3	5	10				9				8	7			11*	6	12		4		27
1	2		3	5	10	12			9				8	7				6	11		4*		28
1	2		3	5	10				9				8	7				6	11		4		29
1	2		3	5	10				9				8	7				6	11		4		30
1	2		3	5	10	12			9				8*	7				6	11		4		31
1	2		3	5	10	7*			9				8·					6	11	12	4		32
1	2		3	5	10				9*	13			8		12			6	11†	7	4		33
1	2		3	5	10				9				8	7				6	11		4		34
30	34	26	30	31	29	21	18	18	28	7	7		21	19	9	1	5	18	7	4	8	3	
	2				1		3		1	1	2	4	1		3	1	1		1		6	3	
		3	6	1	3	4		4	14	1	4		8	7				4	7	1			

21

1974-75

1	Aug	31	(a)	Ayr U	D	1-1	Jardine (pen)	16,000
2	Sep	7	(h)	Partick T	W	3-2	Fyfe 2, Young	20,000
3		14	(a)	Celtic	W	2-1	Jackson, McDougall	60,000
4		21	(h)	Dumbarton	W	3-2	Johnstone 2, Scott	16,000
5		28	(a)	Kilmarnock	W	6-0	Jardine (pen), Johnstone, McLean, Young 2, McKean	18,000
6	Oct	5	(h)	Morton	W	2-0	Forsyth, McLean	25,000
7		12	(a)	Dunfermline A	W	6-1	Johnstone, Parlane 5	18,000
8		19	(h)	Clyde	W	3-1	Jardine (pen), Johnstone, Fyfe	20,000
9		26	(a)	Hearts	D	1-1	Jardine (pen)	28,000
10	Nov	2	(a)	St. Johnstone	W	2-1	McLean, Young	13,260
11		9	(h)	Dundee	W	1-0	McKean	16,000
12		16	(a)	Motherwell	W	5-0	Johnstone, Parlane, Young, MacDonald, McKean	19,000
13		23	(h)	Hibernian	L	0-1		30,000
14		30	(h)	Dundee U	W	4-2	Jardine 2 (1 pen), McLean, Parlane	25,000
15	Dec	7	(a)	Aberdeen	W	2-1	Johnstone, McLean	25,000
16		14	(h)	Arbroath	W	3-0	Jackson, Parlane 2	20,000
17		21	(a)	Airdrieonians	L	3-4	Jardine 2 (1 pen), Johnstone	20,000
18		28	(h)	Ayr U	W	3-0	Jardine (pen), Johnstone, Parlane	15,000
19	Jan	1	(a)	Partick T	W	4-0	Greig, Jackson, McLean, McDougall	22,000
20		4	(h)	Celtic	W	3-0	Johnstone, McLean, Parlane	70,000
21		11	(a)	Dumbarton	W	5-1	Johnstone, McLean 3, Parlane	16,000
22	Feb	1	(a)	Morton	D	1-1	Fyfe	17,000
23		8	(h)	Dunfermline A	W	2-0	McLean, McDonald	23,000
24		15	(h)	Kilmarnock	D	3-3	Parlane 3	20,000
25		22	(a)	Clyde	W	2-1	O'Hara, McKean	18,000
26	Mar	1	(h)	Hearts	W	2-1	McKean, McLean	32,000
27		8	(h)	St. Johnstone	W	1-0	Smith S (og)	40,000
28		15	(a)	Dundee	W	2-1	McLean, Parlane	22,700
29		22	(h)	Mortherwell	W	3-0	Johnstone 2, Miller	40,000
30		29	(a)	Hibernian	D	1-1	Stein	38,585
31	Apr	5	(a)	Dundee U	D	2-2	Johnstone, McLean	12,000
32		12	(h)	Aberdeen	W	3-2	Johnstone, Miller (pen), Stein	40,000
33		19	(a)	Arbroath	W	2-1	Parlane, Stein	6,392
34		26	(h)	Airdrieonians	L	0-1		60,000

FINAL LEAGUE POSITION : 1st in Division One

Appearances

Sub. Appearances

Goals

Kennedy	Jardine	Miller	Forsyth	Jackson	Johnstone	McLean	Young	Parlane	Fyfe	Scott	MacDonald	Denny	McDougall	Greig	McKean	O'Hara	Hamilton	Stein	No.
1	2	3	4	5	6	7	8	9	10	11									1
1	2	3	6	5	8		7	9	11		10		4						2
1	2		6	5	8	12	7	9	11		10		4*	3					3
1	2		6	5	4	8*	10	12	11†	9	13			3	7				4
1	2		6	5	4	8	11			9	10			3	7				5
1	2		6	5	4	8	11	9			10			3	7				6
1	2		6	5	4	8	11	9		12	10			3*	7				7
1	2	3		5	4	8	11		9		10	6			7				8
1	2		6	5	4	8	11	9*			10			3	7	12			9
1	2		6	5	4	8	11	9			10			3	7				10
1	2		6	5	4	8	11	9			10			3	7				11
1	2		6	5	4*	8	11	9			10		12	3	7				12
1	2		6	5	4*	8	11	9			10		12	3	7				13
1	2*		6	5		8	11	9			10	12	4	3	7				14
1	2		6	5	4	8	11	9			10			3	7				15
1	2			5	4	8	11	9			10	6		3	7				16
1	2			5	4	8	11†	9	13		10	6		3	7*		12		17
1	2	10		5	4	7		9		11		6	8	3					18
1	2	10	6	5	8	7		9		11			4	3					19
1	2	12	6	5*	4	7	13	9		11†	10		8	3					20
1	2			5	8	7	12	9		11*	10	6	4	3					21
1	2	3	6	5		7	11	9	12		10	8*	4						22
1	2	3	6	5		7	11	9			10		4*		12	8			23
1	2	3	6	5	8	7*		9		12			4		11		10		24
1	2	3	6	5		7		9			10		12		8	4	11*		25
1	2	3	6	5	8		11	9			10		4		7				26
1	2		6	5		7	11	9			10			3	4		8		27
1	2	12	6	5		7	11	9			10			3*	4		8		28
1	2	3	6	5	11	7*	12	9			10				4		8		29
1	2*	3	6	5	11	7		9			10		12		4		8		30
1	2	3	6	5	11	7*	13	9			10				4	12	8†		31
1	2	3	6	5	11	7*		9	12		10				4		8		32
1	2	3	6	5	11	7*	13	9	12		10				4		8†		33
1	2	12	6	5	11	7	13	9			10			3	4*		8†		34
34	34	15	30	33	27	32	22	30	6	7	29	6	11	21	25	2	2	8	
	3				1	6	1	4	2	1	1		3	1	1	2	1		
	9	2	1	3	15	14	5	17	4	1	2			2	1	5	1	3	

23

1975-76

1	Aug	30	(h)	Celtic	W	2-1	Johnstone, Young	69,000
2	Sep	6	(a)	Hearts	W	2-0	Anderson (og), Murray (og)	25,000
3		13	(h)	St. Johnstone	W	2-0	Johnstone, Stein	25,000
4		20	(h)	Hibernian	D	1-1	Blackley (og)	37,000
5		27	(a)	Dundee	D	0-0		15,087
6	Oct	4	(h)	Aberdeen	W	1-0	McDougall	22,000
7		11	(a)	Ayr U	L	0-3		15,000
8		18	(a)	Motherwell	L	1-2	Johnstone	18,925
9	Nov	1	(a)	Celtic	D	1-1	Parlane	55,000
10		8	(h)	Hearts	L	1-2	Henderson	24,000
11		12	(h)	Dundee U	W	4-1	Jackson, McDonald, Forsyth, Parlane	10,000
12		15	(a)	St. Johnstone	W	5-1	Jardine, McLean, Parlane, McKean, MacDonald (og)	9,500
13		22	(a)	Hibernian	L	1-2	Young	26,547
14		29	(h)	Dundee	W	2-1	Henderson 2	15,000
15	Dec	6	(a)	Aberdeen	L	0-1		19,565
16		13	(h)	Ayr U	W	3-0	Jardine (pen), McKean, Henderson	20,000
17		20	(h)	Motherwell	W	3-2	Johnstone 2, Henderson	20,000
18		27	(a)	Dundee U	D	0-0		11,500
19	Jan	1	(h)	Celtic	W	1-0	Johnstone	57,839
20		3	(a)	Hearts	W	2-1	Henderson 2	23,000
21		10	(h)	St. Johnstone	W	4-0	Miller (pen), Johnstone, McKean, Hamilton	18,000
22		17	(h)	Hibernian	W	2-0	McLean, Parlane	40,000
23		31	(a)	Dundee	D	1-1	Johnstone	14,407
24	Feb	7	(h)	Aberdeen	W	2-1	MacDonald, Henderson	20,000
25		21	(a)	Ayr U	W	1-0	McKean	15,000
26		28	(a)	Motherwell	W	1-0	Johnstone	25,241
27	Mar	20	(h)	Hearts	W	3-1	Jackson, Johnstone, McLean	30,000
28		27	(a)	St. Johnstone	W	3-0	Grieg, Johnstone 2	9,079
29	Apr	3	(a)	Hibernian	W	3-0	MacDonald, Johnstone, Henderson	18,820
30		10	(h)	Dundee	W	3-0	Greig, Johnstone, McKean	25,000
31		14	(a)	Aberdeen	D	0-0		17,968
32		17	(h)	Ayr U	W	2-1	MacDonald, Parlane	25,000
33		21	(h)	Motherwell	W	2-1	McLean, Henderson	27,000
34		24	(a)	Dundee U	W	1-0	Johnstone	17,000
35		26	(a)	Celtic	D	0-0		51,000
36	May	4	(h)	Dundee U	D	0-0		40,000

FINAL LEAGUE POSITION : 1st in Premier Division

Appearances

Sub. Appearances

Goals

McCloy	Jardine	Greig	Forsyth	Jackson	MacDonald	McLean	McKean	Stein	Johnstone	Young	O'Hara	Miller	Parlane	Denny	Fyfe	Dawson	McDougall	Scott	Kennedy	Henderson	Hamilton	Boyd	
1	2*	3	4	5	6	7	8	9	10	11	12												1
1		3	4*	5	6	7	8†	13	10	11		2	9	12									2
1	2	4		5	6		7*	13	10	11	8	3	9†	12									3
1		4		5	6	7*	8	13	10	11†		3	9	2	12								4
1		4		5	6	7			10	11		2	9		3	8							5
1	2	4		5		7			10	11		6	9		3	8							6
1	2	4		5	6	7	13		10			12	9†		3	8*	11						7
1	2	3	4	5	6	7	8		10	11			9										8
	2	3	4	5	6	7	8		10	11			9					1					9
	2	3	4	5	6	12	8		13				9		7*				1	11	10†		10
		4	10	6	5	12	7	8*	11†			3	9	2					1	13			11
		4	3	6	5	10	7	8	11				9	2					1				12
		4	3	6	5	10	7	8*	11	12			9†	2					1	13			13
	2	3	4	5	6	10	7		11										1	9	8		14
	2	3	4	5	6	10	7		11										1	9	8		15
	2	3	4	5	6	10	7		11										1	9	8		16
	2*	3	4	5	6	10	7		11			12							1	9	8		17
		3	4*	5	6	10	7		11			2		12					1	9	8		18
		3	4	5	6	10	7*		11		13	2					12		1	9	8†		19
1		3	4	5	6	10	7		11		12	2								9	8*		20
1		3	4	5	6	10	7		11			2								9	8		21
1		3	4	5	6	10	7					2	11							9	8		22
1		3	4	5	6	10	7		11			2	9*							12	8		23
1	12	3	4	5	6	10	7		11			2	13							9†	8*		24
1	12	3	4	5	6	10	7					2	11							9	8*		25
1	13	3	4	5	6	7*	10		11			2	12							9	8†		26
1		3	4	5	6	10	7		11			2								9	8		27
1	12	3	4	5	6	10	7*		11			2	13							9†	8		28
1		3	4	5	6	10	7		11			2	12							9*	8		29
1	13	3	4	5	6	10†	7		11			2	12							9	8*		30
1	13	3	4	5	6	10†	7*		11			2	12							9	8		31
1	12	3	4	5*	6	10	7		11			2	13							9†	8		32
1	4	3	5*		6	10	7		11			2		12						9	8		33
1	8	4		5	6	10	7		11			3		2						9			34
1	2	4			6	10	7		5			3	11							9	8		35
		4	3		6	10	7					2	11	5*			12		1	9	8		36
24	18	36	28	33	34	34	32	3	32	7	1	25	17	6	1	3	3	1	12	23	22	1	
	7			1	1	1	3	1	1	3	2	7	3	2		1	1		3				
2	2	1	2	4	4	5	1	15	2		1	5					1			10	1		

1976-77

1	Sep	4	(a)	Celtic	D	2-2	Johnstone, Parlane	57,000
2		11	(h)	Kilmarnock	D	0-0		25,000
3		18	(a)	Hibernian	D	1-1	Parlane	19,606
4		25	(h)	Hearts	W	4-2	Hamilton, Miller (pen), Johnstone, Parlane	20,000
5	Oct	2	(a)	Ayr U	D	1-1	Parlane	14,000
6		16	(h)	Aberdeen	W	1-0	MacDonald	26,000
7		23	(a)	Motherwell	L	1-3	Hamilton	15,857
8		30	(a)	Partick T	L	1-2	Watson	20,000
9	Nov	9	(h)	Dundee U	W	3-0	Parlane, Jackson, McKean	16,000
10		13	(a)	Kilmarnock	W	4-0	Parlane, McKean, Jackson 2	14,700
11		20	(h)	Hibernian	D	1-1	Parlane	24,000
12		24	(h)	Celtic	L	0-1		50,000
13		27	(a)	Hearts	W	1-0	Parlane	19,000
14	Dec	26	(h)	Motherwell	W	1-0	O'Hara	25,000
15	Jan	1	(h)	Partick T	W	1-0	Johnstone	19,000
16		8	(h)	Kilmarnock	W	3-0	O'Hara, Parlane 2	22,000
17		11	(a)	Celtic	L	0-1		52,000
18		19	(a)	Aberdeen	D	3-3	Johnstone, MacDonald, Miller (pen)	21,000
19		22	(h)	Hearts	W	3-2	Johnstone, MacDonald 2	22,000
20	Feb	5	(a)	Ayr U	W	2-0	Johnstone, McLean	12,800
21		12	(h)	Dundee U	L	2-3	Jackson, MacDonald	16,000
22		16	(a)	Hibernian	D	0-0		12,452
23		19	(h)	Aberdeen	W	1-0	Miller (pen)	14,000
24	Mar	5	(a)	Motherwell	W	2-0	Watson, MacDonald	15,468
25		8	(a)	Dundee U	D	0-0		10,500
26		15	(a)	Partick T	L	3-4	Watson, Johnstone, Parlane	12,000
27		19	(h)	Celtic	D	2-2	Parlane 2	55,000
28		23	(h)	Ayr U	D	1-1	Johnstone	7,000
29		26	(a)	Kilmarnock	L	0-1		8,000
30	Apr	2	(h)	Hibernian	W	2-1	Parlane, Johnstone	10,000
31		9	(a)	Hearts	W	3-1	Parlane, Johnstone, Jardine (pen)	12,500
32		13	(h)	Partick T	W	2-1	Johnstone, Jardine (pen)	3,500
33		16	(h)	Ayr U	W	5-1	Johnstone, MacDonald 2, Miller (pen), Hamilton	10,000
34		20	(h)	Motherwell	W	4-1	Johnstone, Robertson (pen), Parlane, MacDonald	5,000
35		23	(a)	Dundee U	W	1-0	Johnstone	8,000
36		30	(a)	Aberdeen	L	1-2	Johnstone	13,484

FINAL LEAGUE POSITION : 2nd in Premier Division

Appearances

Sub. Appearances

Goals

#	McCloy	Miller	Greig	Forsyth	Denny	MacDonald	McLean	Jardine	Parlane	Munro	Johnstone	Henderson	McKean	Jackson	Watson	Hamilton	Kennedy	O'Hara	Robertson	McDougall	Dawson	Steele	Stein	Morris	Armour	#
1	1	2	3	4	5	6	7	8	9	10	11															1
2	1	2	3	4	5	6	7*	8	13	10	11	9†	12													2
3	1		3	4	5	6	7	2	9		11		10			8										3
4	1		3	4		6	7	2	9	10	11			5		8										4
5	1		3	4		6	7*	2	9	10	11		12	5		8										5
6			3	4	6	10	7	2	9		11†	13	12	5		8*	1									6
7			3	4			7*	2	9		11		13	5	6	8†	1		12	10						7
8			3	4	6	10	7	2	9		11			5		8*	1		12							8
9		12	3			10	7	2	9		11			5*	6	8	1					4				9
10		12	3			10	7	2	9		11			5*	6	8	1					4				10
11		12	3			10	7	2	9		11			5	6	8*	1					4				11
12			3			10	7	2	9		11*			5	6	8	1					4	12			12
13			3			10	7	2	9					5	6	8	1					4		11		13
14		12	3	4			7	2	9*	10	11			5	6		1	8								14
15			3	4		10	7	2	9*		11			5	6		1	8	12							15
16			3	4		10	7	2	9		11		12	5*	6		1	8								16
17			3	4		10	7	2	9		11			5	6		1	8								17
18		12	3	4		10	7	2	9†		11		13	5	6		1	8*								18
19			3	4		10	7*	2			11		12	5	6	8	1		9							19
20		12	3	4		10	7	2			11			5	6	8*	1		9							20
21		12	3	4*		10	7	2			11		13	5	6	8	1		9†							21
22			3	4		10	7	2	9		11		12	5*	6	8	1									22
23			3	4		10	7*	2	9		11		12	5	6	8†	1				13					23
24		12	3	4		10	7	2	9†				13	5	6		1	8*	11							24
25			3	4		10	7	2	9					5	6	8	1	11*	12							25
26			3	4		10	7	2	9		11				6	8*	1		12					5		26
27			3	4		10	7	2	9		11			5	6	8	1									27
28			3	4		10	7	2	9		11			5	6	8	1									28
29			3	4		10	7	2	9		11	12		5	6	8*	1									29
30			3	4		10	7	2	9		11			5	6	8	1									30
31			3	4		10	7	2	9*		11		12	5	6	8	1									31
32			3	4		10	7	2	9		11			5	6	8	1									32
33		3		4		10	7	2	9		11		12	5*	6	8	1									33
34		3		4		10	7	2	9					5	6	8	1		11							34
35		3*		4		10	7	2	9				12	5	6	8	1		11							35
36			3	4		10	7	2	9		11			5	6*	8	1							12		36
	5	17	30	25	5	29	36	36	31	3	27	4	14	30	30	22	31	5	7	1	1	5	1	1		
		7			1				2	2			3	8				1	4	3			1	1		
		4	2			9	1	4	16		15		2		3	3		2	1							

1977-78

1	Aug	13	(a)	Aberdeen	L	1-3	Russell	22,000
2		20	(h)	Hibernian	L	0-2		20,000
3		27	(a)	Partick T	W	4-0	Smith 2, Miller (pen), Russell	18,584
4	Sep	10	(h)	Celtic	W	3-2	Smith 2, Johnstone	48,788
5		17	(a)	St. Mirren	D	3-3	Jardine, Johnstone, Cooper	25,000
6		24	(h)	Ayr U	W	2-0	Smith 2	18,000
7	Oct	1	(h)	Clydebank	W	4-1	Smith 2, Cooper 2	15,000
8		8	(a)	Dundee U	W	1-0	Russell	17,316
9		15	(a)	Motherwell	W	4-1	Smith, Johnstone 3	20,050
10		22	(h)	Aberdeen	W	3-1	Smith, Jardine (pen), MacDonald	35,000
11		29	(a)	Hibernian	W	1-0	Jardine (pen)	22,590
12	Nov	5	(h)	Partick T	D	3-3	Parlane 2, MacDonald	25,000
13		12	(a)	Celtic	D	1-1	Johnstone	56,000
14		19	(h)	St. Mirren	W	2-1	Johnstone, Miller (pen)	21,000
15		26	(a)	Ayr U	W	5-0	Parlane, Johnstone 3, Jackson	15,300
16	Dec	10	(h)	Dundee U	W	2-0	McLean, Smith	25,000
17		17	(h)	Motherwell	W	3-1	Smith 2, Johnstone	23,000
18		24	(a)	Aberdeen	L	0-4		21,000
19		31	(h)	Hibernian	D	0-0		25,000
20	Jan	2	(a)	Partick T	W	2-1	Smith, Johnstone	30,000
21		7	(h)	Celtic	W	3-1	Smith, Greig, Parlane	51,000
22		14	(a)	St. Mirren	W	2-0	Smith, Johnstone	24,300
23	Feb	4	(h)	Clydebank	W	1-0	Johnstone	18,000
24		19	(a)	Clydebank	W	3-0	Cooper, Johnstone 2	8,000
25		25	(a)	Motherwell	W	5-3	Cooper, Johnstone 2, Smith, McVie (og)	20,387
26	Mar	4	(h)	Aberdeen	L	0-3		40,000
27		21	(h)	Partick T	W	2-1	Jardine, MacDonald	16,000
28		25	(a)	Celtic	L	0-2		50,000
29		29	(a)	Hibernian	D	1-1	Parlane	21,245
30	Apr	1	(h)	St. Mirren	D	1-1	Johnstone	20,000
31		8	(a)	Ayr U	W	5-2	Smith 2, Greig, Johnstone 2	13,400
32		12	(h)	Ayr U	D	1-1	Johnstone	15,000
33		15	(a)	Clydebank	W	2-0	Johnstone 2	10,000
34		19	(a)	Dundee U	W	1-0	Johnstone	17,293
35		22	(h)	Dundee U	W	3-0	Cooper, Jackson, Jardine (pen)	25,000
36		29	(h)	Motherwell	W	2-0	Smith, Jackson	40,000

FINAL LEAGUE POSITION : 1st in Premier Division

Appearances

Sub. Appearances

Goals

McCloy	Jardine	Miller	Forsyth	Jackson	MacDonald	McKay	Russell	Parlane	Robertson	Cooper	McKean	McLean	Smith	Johnstone	Greig	Watson	Kennedy	Dawson	Hamilton	No.
1	2	3	4	5	6	7*	8	9	10	11	12									1
1	2	3	4	5	6		8	9	10	11*		7	12							2
1	2	3	4	5	6		8			11		7	10	9						3
1	2	3	4		6*		8	9†		11	7	12	10	5	13					4
1	2	12	4	5			8			11		7	10	9	3*	6				5
	2	3	4	5	6		8			11		7	10	9			1			6
	2	3	4	5	6		8			11	7*	12	10	9			1			7
	2	3	4	5	6		8			11		7	10	9			1			8
		3	4	5	6		8			11		7	10	9	2		1			9
	2		4	5	6		8			11		7	10	9	3		1			10
	2		4	5	6		8			11		7	10	9	3		1			11
	2		4	5*	6		8	9	12	11		7	10		3		1			12
	2		4	5	6		8			11		7	10	9	3		1			13
	2	3		5	6		8	12		11		7	10*	9	4		1			14
	2	3		5	6		8	13		11	12	7*	10†	9	4		1			15
	2	3		5*	6		8	12		11	13	7†	10	9	4		1			16
	2		4	5	6		8			11		7	10	9	3		1			17
	2		4	5	6		8	12		11		7	10*	9	3		1			18
	2		4	5	6		8	12		11		7	10	9*	3		1			19
	2	3	4	5	6		8	12		11*		7	10	9			1			20
	2	12	4	5	6		8	13		11†		7*	10	9	3		1			21
	2		4	5	6		8			11		7	10	9	3		1			22
1	2		4	5	6		8	13		11†	12	7*	10	9	3					23
	2			5	6		8			11		7	10	9	4		1	3		24
	2		4	5	6		8	12		11		7*	10	9	3		1			25
	2		4	5	6		8*	13		11		7	10†	9	3		1	12		26
	2	13	4	5	6			12		11		7*	10	9	3		1		8†	27
	2	12	4	5	6		8*	13		11†		7	10	9	3		1			28
1	2	12	4	5	6					11		7*	10	9	3				8	29
1	2	13	4	5	6					11	12	7*	10	9	3				8†	30
1	2	13	4	5	6		8†	12		11		7*	10	9	3					31
1	2	13	4	5	6		8†	12		11		7*	10	9	3					32
1	2		4	5	6		8*	13		11		7	10†	9	3				12	33
1	2		4	5			8			11		7	10	9	3	6				34
1	2		4	5	6		8	12		11		7*	10†	9	3				13	35
1	2		4	5	6		8			11		7*	10	9	3				12	36
14	32	16	31	35	34	1	33	6	2	34	6	29	34	33	28	2	22	1	3	
	8						16	1	1	4	2	1			1	2	1	1		
		5	2		3	3		3	5		6		1	20	25	2				

1978-79

1	Aug	12	(h)	St. Mirren	L	0-1		28,000
2		19	(a)	Hibernian	D	0-0		23,000
3		26	(h)	Partick T	D	0-0		28,000
4	Sep	9	(a)	Celtic	L	1-3	Parlane	60,000
5		16	(h)	Aberdeen	D	1-1	Forsyth A (pen)	25,000
6		23	(a)	Morton	D	2-2	Parlane, Johnstone	16,500
7		30	(h)	Motherwell	W	4-1	Smith 2, McLean, Johnstone	25,000
8	Oct	7	(h)	Dundee U	D	1-1	MacDonald	27,000
9		14	(a)	Hearts	D	0-0		18,159
10		21	(a)	St. Mirren	W	1-0	Forsyth A (pen)	22,000
11		28	(h)	Hibernian	W	2-1	Smith, Forsyth A (pen)	25,000
12	Nov	4	(a)	Partick T	L	0-1		21,000
13		11	(h)	Celtic	D	1-1	Forsyth A (pen)	53,000
14		18	(a)	Aberdeen	D	0-0		26,000
15		25	(h)	Morton	W	3-0	Smith, Johnstone, Cooper	22,000
16	Dec	9	(a)	Dundee U	L	0-3		15,247
17		16	(h)	Hearts	W	5-3	Watson, Johnstone 4	18,000
18		23	(h)	St. Mirren	W	1-0	Johnstone	20,000
19	Jan	20	(a)	Morton	W	2-0	Watson, MacDonald	18,000
20	Feb	10	(h)	Dundee U	W	1-0	Robertson	22,000
21		24	(a)	Hearts	L	2-3	Smith, Parlane	18,000
22	Mar	14	(h)	Hibernian	W	1-0	Smith	15,000
23		17	(a)	Partick T	W	2-0	Cooper, Urquhart	18,665
24		27	(a)	St. Mirren	W	2-1	Urquhart 2	20,000
25	Apr	7	(h)	Morton	D	1-1	Cooper	18,000
26		10	(h)	Motherwell	W	3-0	Smith, Cooper, MacDonald	8,000
27		14	(a)	Motherwell	L	0-2		14,612
28		21	(a)	Dundee U	W	2-1	Smith, Dawson	20,264
29		25	(a)	Aberdeen	L	1-2	Smith	17,000
30		28	(h)	Hearts	W	4-0	Russell 3, Parlane	21,000
31	May	2	(a)	Motherwell	W	2-1	Smith, Jackson	13,052
32		5	(h)	Celtic	W	1-0	MacDonald	52,841
33		7	(h)	Aberdeen	W	2-0	Smith, Cooper	28,000
34		21	(a)	Celtic	L	2-4	Russell, MacDonald	52,000
35		23	(h)	Partick T	W	1-0	Johnstone	2,000
36		31	(a)	Hibernian	L	1-2	Urquhart	4,000

FINAL LEAGUE POSITION : 2nd in Premier Division

Appearances

Sub. Appearances

Goals

McCloy	Jardine	Forsyth A	Forsyth T	Jackson	MacDonald	McLean	Russell	Johnstone	Smith	Watson	Urquhart	Parlane	Miller	Cooper	Dawson	Robertson	McDonald	Armour	McKay	Morris	Strickland	No.
1	2	3	4	5	6	7	8	9	10	11*	12											1
1	2	3	4		6	7	8	5	10		11*	9	12									2
1	2	3		4		7	8	5	10	6		9		11								3
1	2	3	4	5	6*	7†	8		10	11		9	12	13								4
1	2	3	4	5	6	7	8		10	11		9										5
1	2	3	4	5	6	7	8		10	11		9										6
1	2	3	4	5*	6	7†	8		10	11		9	12	13								7
1	2	3	4		6	7	8		10	11		9*	5	12								8
1	2	3	4	5	6	7	8		10	11		9*		12								9
1	2	3	4		6	7	8	5	10*			9	12	11								10
1	2	3	4		6	7	8	5	10			9	12	11*								11
1	2	3	4		6	7	8	5	10	13	12	9*		11†								12
1	2	3	4		6	7	8	5	9	10				11								13
1	2			5	6	7	8	4	10	11		9			3							14
1	4	2		5		7	8	9	10	6				11	3							15
1	4	2		5	6	7	8*	9	10	12		13		11†	3							16
1	4			5	6	7	8	9	12	10			2	11*	3							17
1	4			5	6	7	8	9		10			2	11	3							18
1	2		4	5	6	7	8	9		10				11	3							19
1	2		4	5	6	7	8	9	13	10*				11†	3	12						20
1	2		4	5	6	7	8		10			9		11*	3		12					21
1	2		4	5	6	7	8		10			9		11	3							22
1	2		4	5	6	7	8		10			9		11	3							23
1	2			5	6	7	8	4	10			9	12	11*	3							24
1	4			5	6	7	8		10	9	12		2*	11	3							25
1	4			5	6	7	8	9	10				2	11	3							26
1	4			5	6	7*	8†	9	10	13			2	11	3	12						27
1	4			5	10	12	8	6	11			9	2	7*	3							28
1	4				6	7	8	5	10	12		9	2*	11	3							29
1	2			5	6	7*	8	4	10			9		11	3			12				30
1	2			5	6	7	8	4	10			9		11	3							31
1	2			5	6	7	8	4	10			9		11	3							32
1	2			5	6	7	8	4	10			9		11	3							33
1	2			5	6	7*	8	4	10			9	12	11	3							34
1	2			5*	6	7	8	4	10			9†	12	11	3		13					35
1		2						9	10	6	8	4		11†	3	13			12	5	7*	36
36	35	16	17	28	33	34	36	31	31	11	6	21	10	26	23					1	1	
									11	2	2	4	3	7	4	2	2	2	1			
	4			1	5	1	4	9	11	2	4	4		5	1	1						

1979-80

1	Aug	11	(a)	Hibernian	W	3-1	MacDonald A, Cooper, Russell		17,731
2		18	(h)	Celtic	D	2-2	MacDonald J, Russell		29,767
3		25	(a)	Partick T	L	1-2	Johnstone		20,000
4	Sep	8	(h)	St. Mirren	W	3-1	Johnstone, Smith, Miller (pen)		23,000
5		15	(a)	Aberdeen	L	1-3	Johnstone		23,000
6		22	(h)	Dundee	W	2-0	McGeachie (og), Glennie (og)		24,000
7		29	(a)	Kilmarnock	L	1-2	Johnstone		14,000
8	Oct	6	(a)	Dundee U	D	0-0			19,464
9		13	(h)	Morton	D	2-2	Johnstone 2		25,000
10		20	(h)	Hibernian	W	2-0	Smith, Miller (pen)		20,000
11		27	(a)	Celtic	L	0-1			56,000
12	Nov	3	(h)	Partick T	W	2-1	Urquhart 2		17,000
13		10	(a)	St. Mirren	L	1-2	Forsyth A		17,362
14		17	(h)	Aberdeen	L	0-1			18,000
15		24	(a)	Dundee	L	1-3	Jackson		13,342
16	Dec	1	(h)	Kilmarnock	W	2-1	Johnstone, Russell		15,000
17		8	(a)	Morton	W	1-0	Johnstone		15,000
18		15	(h)	Dundee U	W	2-1	Johnstone, Kopel (og)		20,000
19		22	(a)	Hibernian	L	1-2	McLean		18,740
20		29	(h)	Celtic	D	1-1	Johnstone		36,000
21	Jan	5	(h)	St. Mirren	L	1-2	Jardine (pen)		17,000
22		12	(a)	Aberdeen	L	2-3	MacDonald J, Jackson		19,500
23	Feb	23	(h)	Morton	W	3-1	Russell, Smith, MacDonald J		25,000
24	Mar	1	(h)	Hibernian	W	1-0	Johnstone		30,000
25		12	(h)	Dundee	W	1-0	Stevens		15,000
26		15	(h)	Partick T	D	0-0			22,000
27		19	(a)	Dundee U	D	0-0			9,533
28		29	(h)	Aberdeen	D	2-2	Jardine (pen), MacDonald J		20,000
29	Apr	2	(a)	Celtic	L	0-1			52,000
30		5	(a)	Dundee	W	4-1	Cooper, Johnstone 2, Smith		12,948
31		19	(a)	Morton	W	1-0	Russell		14,000
32		23	(a)	Kilmarnock	L	0-1			8,500
33		26	(h)	Dundee U	W	2-1	Jardine (pen), McLean		16,000
34		30	(h)	Kilmarnock	W	1-0	MacDonald J		8,000
35	May	3	(a)	Partick T	L	3-4	Russell 2, Johnstone		15,000
36		7	(a)	St. Mirren	L	1-4	Miller		3,000

FINAL LEAGUE POSITION : 5th in Premier Division

Appearances

Sub. Appearances

Goals

McCloy	Miller	Dawson	Jardine	Jackson	Watson	McLean	Russell	Johnstone	MacDonald A	Cooper	Smith	MacDonald J	Stevens	Parlane	Forsyth A	Urquhart	Mackay	Dalziel	Forsyth T	Young	Redford	#
1	2	3	4	5	6	7	8	9	10	11												1
1	2	3	4	5	6		8*	9	10	7	12	11										2
1	2	3	4	5	6*	7†	8	9	10	11	12	13										3
1	12	3	2	5	6	7†	8	9	10	11	13		4*									4
1	13	3*	2	5	6	12	8	9	10†	7	11		4									5
1	2	3	4	5	12	7		9	8*	11	10		6									6
1	8	3	2	5	12	7†		9	6*	11	10	13	4									7
1		3	2	5	6	7		9	8	11			4	10								8
1	8		2	5				9	6	7	11		4		3	10						9
1	8		2	5*		12		9	6	7	11		4		3	10						10
1	2		4		6	7*		9	8	11	12		5		3	10						11
1	7		2	5*	6			9	8	11	12	13	4		3	10†						12
1	8†	3	5		6*	7		9	10			13	4		2		12	11				13
1	8*	3	5		6	7		9	10		11	12	4		2							14
1		3	4	5	12	7*	13	9	8		10†	11	6		2							15
1		3	2	5		7	8	9	10	11			6					4				16
1		3	2	5		7	8	9	10	12	11*		6					4				17
		3	2	5		7*	8	9	10	12	13	11†	6					4	1			18
		3	2	5	10	7		9†	8*	13	12	11	6					4	1			19
1	12	3	2	5		7	8*	9	10		11		6					4				20
1		3	2	5		7	8		10	12	9†	11	6*	13				4				21
1	3*		2	5		7†	8		10	13	12	11	6	9				4				22
1		3	2				8	9		7	6	11	4					5		10		23
1		3	2				8*	9	12	7	4	11	6					5		10		24
1		3	2	5			8	9		7	12	11*	6					4		10		25
1		3	2	5		13	8*	9	12†	7	11		6					4		10		26
1		3	2	5				9*	12	7	8	11	6					4		10		27
1		3	2	5		7	8	9	10	11			6					4				28
1	8	3	2	5				9		7	6	11						4		10		29
1		3	2	5	12		8	9		7	6	11*						4		10		30
1		3	2	5	12		8	9		7	4*	11	6							10		31
1		3	2	5	12		8	9*		7	4	11	6							10		32
1		3	2	5		7	8	9			4	11	6							10		33
1	12	3	2			7	8	13	9		4*	11	6						5†	10		34
1	13	3	2	5		7†	8	4	9	12	11		6*							10		35
1	9		2	5	11	7		12	4	8†	6*			3		13				10		36
34	13	32	35	29	12	22	22	31	23	25	20	21	31	2	8	4	1	16	2	13		
	5			3	6	1	2	3	5	10	5			1		2						
	3		3	2		2	7	14	1	2	4	5	1		1	2						

33

1980-81

#	Month	Date		Opponent	Result		Scorers	Attendance
1	Aug	9	(a)	Airdrieonians	D	1-1	MacDonald	16,000
2		16	(h)	Partick T	W	4-0	Cooper, McAdam, MacDonald, Jardine	26,000
3		23	(a)	Celtic	W	2-1	Bett, Miller	58,000
4	Sep	6	(a)	Dundee U	W	4-2	Cooper, McAdam, MacDonald, Hegarty(og)	15,000
5		13	(h)	Aberdeen	D	1-1	McAdam	32,000
6		20	(a)	Kilmarnock	W	8-1	MacDonald 3, Redford 2 (1 pen), McAdam, Jardine, Bett	20,000
7		27	(h)	St. Mirren	W	2-0	Bett, Cooper	25,000
8	Oct	4	(a)	Morton	D	2-2	Miller (pen), McAdam	15,000
9		11	(h)	Hearts	W	3-1	McAdam 2, Jefferies (og)	23,700
10		18	(h)	Airdrieonians	D	0-0		22,000
11		25	(a)	Partick T	D	1-1	McAdam	14,000
12	Nov	1	(h)	Celtic	W	3-0	McAdam 2, MacDonald	53,000
13		8	(a)	St. Mirren	D	0-0		17,000
14		15	(h)	Kilmarnock	W	2-0	Johnston, Jardine	16,000
15		22	(a)	Hearts	D	0-0		16,000
16		29	(h)	Morton	L	0-1		16,000
17	Dec	13	(a)	Aberdeen	L	0-2	.	20,000
18		20	(a)	Kilmarnock	D	1-1	Russell	9,500
19	Jan	1	(h)	Partick T	D	1-1	McAdam	17,000
20		3	(a)	Airdrieonians	D	1-1	Dawson	12,000
21		10	(a)	Morton	W	2-0	MacDonald, Redford	13,000
22		31	(h)	Aberdeen	W	1-0	Johnstone	32,500
23	Feb	7	(a)	Dundee U	L	1-2	MacDonald	14,328
24		21	(a)	Celtic	L	1-3	Johnstone	52,800
25		28	(h)	Airdrieonians	W	2-0	MacDonald, Redford	12,200
26	Mar	14	(a)	Hearts	L	1-2	Redford	11,500
27		18	(h)	Dundee U	L	1-4	McAdam	12,000
28		21	(h)	Kilmarnock	W	2-0	Redford, Russell	8,500
29		28	(a)	St. Mirren	L	1-2	Dawson	9,988
30	Apr	1	(h)	Morton	W	4-0	Johnstone 2, MacDonald, Redford	2,500
31		4	(h)	Dundee U	W	2-1	Russell, Redford	14,000
32		15	(h)	St. Mirren	W	1-0	Russell	7,000
33		18	(h)	Celtic	L	0-1		34,000
34		22	(a)	Aberdeen	D	0-0		15,000
35		25	(a)	Partick T	D	1-1	Russell	9,000
36	May	2	(h)	Hearts	W	4-0	Bett, Redford, Russell, Johnston	7,000

FINAL LEAGUE POSITION : 3rd in Premier Division

Appearances

Sub. Appearances

Goals

McCloy	Jardine	Forsyth A	Forsyth T	Jackson	Bett	Cooper	Russell	McAdam	Redford	MacDonald J	Johnston	Johnstone	McLean	Dawson	Miller	Stevens	McKay	Clark	Stewart	
1	2	3	4	5	6	7	8	9	10	11										1
1	2		4	5	6	7*	8	9	3	11	10†	12	13							2
1	2		4	5	6	12	8*	9	10	11†	7	13		3						3
1	2	4*	5	6	11		9	10	8			7		3	12					4
1	2	4*	5	6	7		9	10	13	11	12	8†		3						5
1	2	12	5*	6	11		9†	10	8	13	4	7		3						6
1	2	13	5	6	11		9†	10	8	12	4*	7		3						7
1	2		5	6	7*		9	10	11†	13	4	8		3	12					8
1	2	12	5	6	7*		9	10	8	11†	4	13		3						9
1	2	12	5	6	7		9	10	11	13	4*	8†		3						10
1	2	13	5	6	11†	12	9	10	8		4	7*		3						11
1	2		5	6			9	10	8	11	4	7		3						12
1	2	13	5	6		12	9†	10	8	11	4	7*		3						13
1	2	4	5	6		12		10	8*	11†	9	7		3			13			14
1	2		5	6		12	9	10	8	11	4	7*		3						15
1	2	6*	5		7	8	9	10†	11	12	4	13	3	3						16
1			5		12	8	9	6*	10	11	4	7†		3	2		13			17
1	2		5	6	12	8	9		10	11†	4*	7		3			13			18
1	2			6	11†	8	9	10	12		5	7*		3	4		13			19
1	4		5	6		7	8*	9	10†	11			13	3	2	12				20
1	4			6		7	8	9	10	11				3	2	5				21
1	2		5	6	12	8		10	11*	7	9			3	4					22
1	2		5	6	12	8*		10	11	7	9†			3	13	4				23
1	2		5	6	7*	12	9	10	13	11	4			3	8†					24
1	4		5	6	12	8	9	10	11			7*		3	2					25
1	2*		5	6		8	9	10	11		7	4†		3		12	13			26
	13		5	6†	12	8	9	10	11			7		3	2*	4		1		27
	4		5	6	11	8	9	10				7*	12	3	2			1		28
	13		4	5	6	12	8	9	10			7*	11†	3	2			1		29
	4		5	6		8		10	11		9	7		3	2			1		30
	4		5	6		8		10	11*	12	9	7		3	2			1		31
			5	6		8	9	10	11		4	7		3	2			1		32
	13		5	6*		8	9	10	12	11†	4	7		3	2			1		33
	2		5	6		8	11	10			9	7		3	4			1		34
	2		5	6		8	11	10			9	7		3	4			1		35
	2		5	3		7	8	9	10	11		6			4			1		36
26	29	1	15	29	34	17	23	31	35	26	21	23	23	22	24	7		10		
	2			7			8	5			4	6	3	5	1	2	6	1		
	3				4	3	6	12	9	11	2	4		2	2					

1981-82

1	Aug	29	(a)	Partick T	W	1-0	McLean (pen)	16,000
2	Sep	5	(h)	Hibernian	D	2-2	Bett, Cooper	25,000
3		12	(a)	St. Mirren	D	1-1	MacDonald	15,652
4		19	(h)	Celtic	L	0-2		45,000
5	Oct	3	(h)	Airdrieonians	W	4-1	Bett 2, Johnstone, Jardine	12,500
6		10	(h)	Aberdeen	D	0-0		28,000
7		17	(a)	Dundee	W	3-2	Russell, MacDonald 2	11,956
8		24	(h)	Morton	D	1-1	Russell	17,000
9		31	(h)	Partick T	L	0-2		17,000
10	Nov	7	(a)	Hibernian	W	2-1	Bett 2 (1 pen)	14,800
11		11	(a)	Dundee U	L	0-2		16,138
12		14	(h)	St. Mirren	W	4-1	Johnstone, Russell, Bett (pen), Cooper	18,000
13		21	(a)	Celtic	D	3-3	Dalziel, Bett, MacDonald	48,600
14	Dec	5	(a)	Airdrieonians	D	2-2	MacDonald, Russell	14,500
15		19	(h)	Dundee	W	2-1	Bett (pen), McAdam	8,500
16	Jan	9	(h)	Celtic	W	1-0	Bett (pen)	42,000
17		16	(h)	Dundee U	W	2-0	Dalziel, Cooper	18,000
18		30	(h)	Hibernian	D	1-1	Johnstone	15,000
19	Feb	17	(a)	Partick T	L	0-2		6,513
20		20	(a)	Dundee U	D	1-1	Dawson	12,945
21		27	(h)	Morton	W	3-0	MacDonald, Mackay, Dalziel	10,200
22	Mar	10	(a)	St. Mirren	W	3-2	Bett (pen), Johnstone 2	9,000
23		13	(h)	Aberdeen	L	1-3	Johnstone	24,000
24		17	(a)	Morton	D	0-0		4,579
25		20	(h)	Partick T	W	4-1	Johnstone, Russell, Bett (pen), MacDonald	8,000
26		27	(a)	Hibernian	D	0-0		12,390
27		31	(h)	Airdrieonians	W	1-0	MacDonald	3,000
28	Apr	10	(a)	Celtic	L	1-2	Johnstone	49,144
29		14	(a)	Dundee	L	1-3	MacDonald	7,975
30		17	(a)	Airdrieonians	W	1-0	MacDonald	8,000
31		21	(a)	Aberdeen	L	1-3	Johnstone	8,750
32		24	(h)	Dundee U	D	1-1	MacDonald	10,000
33	May	1	(a)	Morton	W	3-1	Russell, MacDonald 2	6,500
34		5	(h)	St. Mirren	W	3-0	MacDonald, McAdam, Redford	4,500
35		8	(h)	Dundee	W	4-0	Dalziel 3, Redford	8,500
36		15	(a)	Aberdeen	L	0-4		18,000

FINAL LEAGUE POSITION : 3rd in Premier Division

Appearances

Sub. Appearances

Goals

McCloy	Jardine	Miller	Stevens	Forsyth T	Bett	Cooper	Russell	McAdam	Johnstone	McLean	Redford	MacDonald	Johnston	Dawson	Black	Jackson	McClelland	Stewart	Davies	Lyall	Mackay	Dalziel	McIntyre	Robertson	
1	2*	3	4	5	6	7	8	9†	10	11	12	13													1
1	2	13	4	5	6	7	8			11	9†	10	12	3*											2
1	2		4		6	7	8	12	9		10*	11		3		5									3
1	2*	6	5	4	8	7		12	9		10	13	11†	3											4
	2		4	5	6	7*	8		9		12	10	11†	3				1			13				5
	2		4	5	6	7	8	9			12	10	11*	3				1							6
	2		4	5	6	7	8	9			12	10	11*	3				1							7
	2				4	6	7	8	9		12	10	11*	3		5		1							8
	2				4	6	7	8	9	13	12	10	11†	3		5*		1							9
1	2		4		6	7	8		9		10	11		3		5									10
1	2*	13	4		6	7	8	12	9		10†	11		3		5									11
1	2	3	4	5	6	7*	8		9		10†	11									12	13			12
1	2	3	4		6	7*	8		9		13	11				5					12	10†			13
	2	3*	4		6	7†	8		9		12	10				5		1			13	11			14
	2	3*	4		6	7	8	13	9		10†	11	12			5		1							15
	2		4		6	7*	8	12	9			11		3		5		1				10			16
	2		4		6	7	8	5	9		12	11		3				1				10*			17
	2					7	8	4	9		6*	11		3				1			12	10			18
	2	3			6	7	8	4			10	11				5		1				9			19
	2	6			10	7*	8	4	9		12	11		3		5		1							20
	2	10†			6	7*	8	4	9			11		3		5		1			12	13			21
	2	10			6	7	8	4	9			11		3		5		1							22
	2	10*			6	7	8	4	9			11	12	3		5		1							23
1	2				6		8		9		10	11		3		5	4					7			24
1	2				6†		8		9		10	11		3	12	5*	4		13			7			25
	4				6		8		9		10*		2	3		5		1	12	11†		7		13	26
	4				6		8	12	10				2	3		5		1		11*		7		9	27
	2				6	7	8		9		10*	11		3		5	4	1				12			28
	2				6	7	8		9		10	11		3		5	4	1							29
	4				6	7	8		9		10		2	3		5		1	11						30
	4				6		8	12	9		10		2	3		5		1	11*			7			31
	4				6*	13	8	10	9		12	11	2	3		5		1				7†			32
	2				6	7	8*	12	9		10	11		3		5	4	1							33
	2	3			6	7	5		9		10	11					4	1				8			34
	2*	3			6	7	5		9		10	11†					4	1	13		12	8			35
	2*	8			6	7		12			10	11		3		5	4	1				9			36
10	36	14	13	12	35	29	32	15	27	2	20	32	6	25	7	21	14	26	1	3	1	14		1	
	2				1		7	1	1		12	3	2		1				3		6	3	1	1	
	1		11	3	6	2	9	1	2		14		1								1	6			

1982-83

1	Sep	4	(a)	Motherwell	D	2-2	Prytz (pen), Redford	19,159
2		11	(h)	Dundee U	D	0-0		25,000
3		18	(h)	Kilmarnock	W	5-0	MacDonald 2, Russell, Johnstone, McClelland	17,000
4		25	(a)	Aberdeen	W	2-1	Johnstone, Prytz	22,000
5	Oct	2	(h)	Dundee	D	1-1	Johnstone	16,000
6		9	(a)	Morton	D	0-0		15,000
7		16	(a)	St. Mirren	D	2-2	Bett, McKinnon	12,121
8		23	(h)	Hibernian	W	3-2	Johnstone 2, McNamara (og)	17,000
9		30	(a)	Celtic	L	2-3	Prytz, Cooper	60,408
10	Nov	6	(h)	Motherwell	W	4-0	Dalziel 2, MacDonald 2	17,000
11		13	(a)	Dundee U	L	2-4	Johnstone, Cooper	16,470
12		20	(a)	Kilmarnock	D	0-0		9,500
13		27	(h)	Aberdeen	L	0-1		24,000
14	Dec	11	(h)	Morton	D	1-1	Prytz (pen)	9,500
15		18	(h)	St. Mirren	W	1-0	MacDonald	10,500
16		27	(a)	Hibernian	D	0-0		16,000
17	Jan	1	(h)	Celtic	L	1-2	Black	44,000
18		3	(a)	Motherwell	L	0-3		11,383
19		8	(h)	Dundee U	W	2-1	Prytz, Kennedy	15,500
20		15	(h)	Kilmarnock	D	1-1	MacDonald	7,000
21		22	(a)	Aberdeen	L	0-2		22,000
22	Feb	5	(h)	Dundee	D	1-1	McPherson	7,000
23		12	(a)	Morton	W	5-0	Bett 2, Kennedy 2, MacDonald	6,900
24		26	(a)	St. Mirren	L	0-1		11,484
25	Mar	2	(a)	Dundee	L	0-1		6,624
26		5	(h)	Hibernian	D	1-1	Dalziel	10,975
27		19	(h)	Motherwell	W	1-0	McClelland	17,000
28		23	(a)	Celtic	D	0-0		51,062
29		26	(a)	Kilmarnock	W	1-0	MacDonald	6,500
30	Apr	2	(a)	Dundee U	L	1-3	Clark	14,142
31		9	(h)	Aberdeen	W	2-1	Redford, Bett	19,800
32		23	(h)	Morton	W	2-0	MacDonald, Redford	9,500
33		30	(h)	St. Mirren	W	4-0	Bett 2 (1 pen), MacDonald, Clark	9,000
34	May	3	(a)	Dundee	L	1-2	Clark	4,788
35		7	(a)	Hibernian	W	2-1	Cooper 2	10,500
36		14	(h)	Celtic	L	2-4	Cooper, Clark	40,000

FINAL LEAGUE POSITION : 4th in Premier Division

Appearances

Sub. Appearances

Goals

Stewart	McKinnon	Dawson	McClelland	Paterson	Bett	Cooper	Prytz	McAdam	Redford	MacDonald	Johnstone	Russell	Stevens	Dalziel	McPherson	Smith	Mackay	Kennedy	Black	Robertson	McCloy	Davies	Lyall	Clark	Bruce	
1	2	3	4	5	6	7	8	9	10	11																1
1	2	3	4	5	6	7*	8		10	11	9	12														2
1	2	3	4	5*	6	7	8		12	11†	9	10					14									3
1	2	3	4	5	6	7	8*		12	11	9	10														4
1	2	3*	4		6	7	8	5	14	11	9	10†										12				5
1	2		4	5	6	11	8*		3	7	9	10		12												6
1	2		4	5	6	7	8		3	11	9	10														7
1	2	12	4		6	7	8*		3	11†	9	10	5						14							8
1	2	3	4		6	7	8*	14	11	12	9	10†	5													9
1	2	3	4		6	7*	8			11	10†	5	9	14			12									10
1	2	3	4		6	7			10	11*	9		5	12	8											11
1	2	3	4		6	7†	8		10	11	9		5*	12			14									12
1	2	3*	4		6	7	8		10	11	9†		14	5	12											13
1	2		4	5	6	7*	8		3		9	10†		12	11				14							14
1	2*		4	5	6	14			3	11†		8		12		7		9	10							15
1	2		4	5	6	12			3	11		8					7*	9	10							16
1	2	3		5	6	7			12	11		8	4						9	10*						17
1	2	3		5	6	7				11		8	4						9	10						18
	2			5	6	12	7		3		11	8*	4					9	10		1					19
	2*			5	6	7	8†		3	11		4	14	12				9	10		1					20
	2	10		5	6	7*	8†		3	11	12	4						9	14		1					21
	2		4		6		8		10	11		7	5					9	3		1					22
	2		4		6		8		10	11		7	5					9	3		1					23
	2		4		6	12	8		10			7	5					9*	3	11	1					24
	2		4		6	12			10†			7	5					9*	3	11	1	8	14			25
	2		4		6	12	8		10	11†		7	5					9	3*		1		14			26
12	2	3		5	6	7*	8†		10	11		4	14								1			9		27
8	2	3		5	6	7	12		10*	11†		4	14								1			9		28
8	2	3		5	6	7			10	11		4									1			9		29
8	2		4	5	6	7			3	11	10*										1		14	9		30
8	2	3		5	6	12			10	11†	7*	4	14								1			9		31
8	2	3		5	6	10†			12	11	7*	4	14								1			9		32
8	2	3		5	6	7	12		10*	11†	12	4									1			9		33
	2	3			6	7	12		10	11	8*	5									1	14	4†	9		34
	2			5	6		8*		10†	11		4						14			1	3		9		35
8*	2	3		5	6	7			10	11†	12	4	14								1			9		36
18	30	24	35	20	35	26	24	2	29	25	18	18	10	7	15	1	2	12	11	2	17	2	2	10	1	
1	1				5	6	2	4	3		3				7	5	1	2	1	4	2		2	2		
1		2		6	5	5	3	10	6	1		3	1				3	1					4			

1983-84

1	Aug	20	(h)	St. Mirren	D	1-1	Prytz (pen)	21,500
2	Sep	3	(a)	Celtic	L	1-2	McCoist	50,662
3		10	(a)	Hearts	L	1-3	Mitchell	16,173
4		17	(h)	Aberdeen	L	0-2		27,500
5		24	(h)	St. Johnstone	W	6-3	McCoist 2, McClelland, Clark, Cooper, Prytz (pen)	12,500
6	Oct	1	(a)	Dundee U	W	2-0	McCoist, Clark	16,738
7		8	(h)	Hibernian	W	1-0	McClelland	21,500
8		15	(a)	Dundee	L	2-3	Russell, Reford	11,945
9		22	(h)	Motherwell	L	1-2	McCoist (pen)	15,000
10		29	(a)	St. Mirren	L	0-3		12,068
11	Nov	5	(h)	Celtic	L	1-2	Clark	40,000
12		12	(a)	Aberdeen	L	0-3		23,000
13		19	(h)	Dundee U	D	0-0		27,800
14		26	(a)	St. Johnstone	W	1-0	Redford	9,740
15	Dec	3	(h)	Hearts	W	3-0	Clark 2, McDonald	22,500
16		10	(a)	Motherwell	W	3-0	McAdam, Cooper, Mitchell	13,586
17		17	(h)	Dundee	W	2-1	Russell, Williamson	16,500
18		27	(a)	Hibernian	W	2-0	Williamson, Cooper	18,251
19		31	(h)	St. Mirren	D	1-1	Clark	21,200
20	Jan	7	(h)	Aberdeen	D	1-1	Cooper (pen)	37,500
21		21	(h)	St. Johnstone	W	2-0	Clark, Russell	17,000
22	Feb	4	(h)	Motherwell	W	2-1	McCoist, Prytz (pen)	17,000
23		11	(a)	Hearts	D	2-2	McCoist, Williamson	18,063
24		25	(a)	Dundee	W	3-1	Russell, Cooper, McPherson	11,750
25	Mar	3	(h)	Hibernian	D	0-0		16,000
26		6	(a)	St. Johnstone	W	4-1	Redford, Clark, Davies, McCoist	5,293
27		31	(a)	Motherwell	W	3-0	Paterson, McPherson, Burns	8,574
28	Apr	2	(a)	Celtic	L	0-3		53,229
29		7	(h)	Hearts	D	0-0		22,000
30		21	(h)	Celtic	W	1-0	Williamson	40,260
31		28	(a)	St. Mirren	D	1-1	Williamson	8,092
32	May	2	(h)	Dundee U	D	2-2	Clark, Williamson	5,000
33		5	(h)	Dundee	D	2-2	Redford, Cooper	17,000
34		9	(a)	Aberdeen	D	0-0		16,200
35		12	(a)	Hibernian	D	0-0		9,134
36		14	(a)	Dundee U	W	2-1	Prytz (pen), McCoist	6,457

FINAL LEAGUE POSITION : 4th in Premier Division

Appearances

Sub. Appearances

Goals

McCloy	Dawson	McClelland	McPherson	Paterson	Redford	Prytz	McCoist	Clark	Russell	Cooper	MacDonald	Davies	MacKinnon	Mitchell	Stewart	Nicholl	Lyall	Stevens	Ferguson	Kennedy	McAdam	Williamson	Walker	Fraser	Mackay	Burns	Munro	Fleck	
1	2	3	4	5*	6†	7	8	9	10	11	12	14																	1
1	3	5	4		6	7	8	9	10				2	11															2
1	2	3	4	5	6*	14	8	9	10†	7			12	11															3
1	2	3	4*	5	12	7†	8	9	10	11	14		6																4
1	2	3	4	5	12	7	8	9	10	11			6*																5
1	2	3	4	5	10	7*	8	9	12	11			6																6
1	2	3	4	5	10*	7	8	9		11			6	12															7
1	2	3	4	5	10*		8	9	7	11	12		6																8
	3	5	4		6	14	8†	9	7*	11	12		2	10	1														9
		4	12		7	8		6*	14	11			9		1	2	3	5	10†										10
1	3	4	6	5	10		7*	9		12	14		8	11†		2													11
1	3	4	6	5	10		7		14	11†			2	9*		8				12									12
1	3	4	6	5	10		8	9	12	11†			2	14		7*													13
1	3	4	8		10	6*	7†	9	12	11			2									14	5						14
1	3	4	10†		6	14		9	7	11	12			8*		2						5							15
1	3	4	10		6			9†	7	11	12			14		2						5	8*						16
1	3	4	10	5*	6			9†	7	11	14		12			2						8							17
	3	4	8	5	6			9†	7	11*	12		2									10	1		14				18
	2	4	10		3	6*		9	7	11	12											5	8†	1	14				19
	3	4	10†		6	14		9*	7	11	12											5	8	1	2				20
		5	8		3	6	12	9*	7		14											4	10†	1	2	11			21
	3	4	12		6	8	10	7	11†				2								5*	9	1		14				22
	3	4	14	5	6	8	10†	7	11	12			2									9*	1						23
1	3	4	5		6	8	10†	9	7*	11			2									14				12			24
	3	4	5		6	8*	10	9†	7	11	14		2										1			12			25
	3	4	5		6	8	10	9†		11	12		14										1	2			7*		26
1	3	4	6	5	14		8*	9	7†	11			2									10				12			27
1	3	4	6	5	12		8	9	7*	11			2									10							28
1	3	4	14	5	6	10	7*	12		11			2									9					8†		29
1		3	4	5	6	8*	10		7	11	14		12									9†							30
1		3	4	5	6	8†	10	12	7*	11	14		2									9							31
1		3	4	5	6		10	9	7	11												8		2					32
1		3	4		6*	8	10†		7	11	12								14			5	9	2					33
1		3	4	5	6		10	9	7	11									12			8*		2					34
1		3	4	5	6*		8	9†	7	11			14									10		2		12			35
	3	5	4		7	8	12	11	10†				2									9*					14	6	36
26	28	36	32	21	28	22	29	27	27	32	2		12	7	2	17	1	1	3		8	16	8	7	1		2	1	
4		4	4	1	3	4	2	15	3	4	5									2	2		1			1	4	3	
	2	2		1	4	4	9	9	4	6	1	1	2								1	6						1	

41

1984-85

1	Aug	11	(h)	St. Mirren	D	0-0		22,398
2		18	(a)	Dumbarton	W	2-1	McCoist, Redford	9,700
3		25	(h)	Celtic	D	0-0		44,000
4	Sep	1	(a)	Dundee	W	2-0	Ferguson I, Redford	14,156
5		8	(h)	Hibernian	W	2-0	Paterson, MacDonald	15,000
6		15	(a)	Aberdeen	D	0-0		22,500
7		22	(h)	Morton	W	2-0	McCoist, Fraser C	15,000
8		29	(h)	Dundee U	W	1-0	Paterson	30,000
9	Oct	6	(a)	Hearts	L	0-1		18,097
10		13	(a)	St. Mirren	W	2-0	Redford, Ferguson I	14,387
11		20	(h)	Dumbarton	D	0-0		16,521
12	Nov	3	(h)	Dundee	D	0-0		14,558
13		10	(a)	Hibernian	D	2-2	Fraser C, Cooper	14,000
14		17	(h)	Aberdeen	L	1-2	Mitchell	44,000
15		24	(a)	Morton	W	3-1	Redford 2, Dawson	11,000
16	Dec	1	(a)	Dundee U	D	1-1	Mitchell	16,477
17		8	(h)	Hearts	D	1-1	Mitchell	12,000
18		15	(h)	St. Mirren	W	2-0	Fraser C, MacDonald	12,763
19		22	(a)	Celtic	D	1-1	Cooper	43,748
20		29	(a)	Dumbarton	W	4-2	Ferguson I, McMinn, Mitchell, Cooper	7,800
21	Jan	1	(h)	Celtic	L	1-2	Cooper	45,000
22		5	(a)	Dundee	D	2-2	Ferguson I 2,	11,911
23		12	(h)	Hibernian	L	1-2	Ferguson I	18,500
24		19	(a)	Aberdeen	L	1-5	Prytz	22,000
25	Feb	2	(h)	Morton	W	2-0	MacDonald, Johnstone	14,121
26		9	(h)	Dundee U	D	0-0		19,370
27		23	(a)	Hearts	L	0-2		14,004
28	Mar	2	(h)	Dumbarton	W	3-1	Ferguson E, McCoist 2	8,424
29		16	(a)	St. Mirren	L	1-2	McCoist	8,608
30		23	(h)	Dundee	L	1-3	McCoist	9,554
31	Apr	6	(h)	Aberdeen	L	1-2	Prytz	23,437
32		20	(a)	Morton	W	3-0	McCoist 3	7,000
33		27	(h)	Hearts	W	3-1	McCoist, Prytz (pen), Cooper	12,193
34	May	1	(a)	Celtic	D	1-1	McCoist (pen)	40,079
35		4	(a)	Dundee U	L	1-2	McCoist	10,251
36		11	(a)	Hibernian	L	0-1		7,149

FINAL LEAGUE POSITION : 4th in Premier Division

Appearances

Sub. Appearances

Goals

Walker	Burns	Dawson	MacKinnon	McClelland	Redford	MacDonald	Fraser C	Ferguson I	McCoist	Cooper	Fraser S	Ferguson E	Paterson	Russell	Clark	McPherson	Mitchell	McCloy	Prytz	McMinn	Fleck	Munro	Ferguson D	Johnstone	Williamson	McFarlane	Bruce	Durrant	
1	2†	3	4	5	6	7*	8	9	10	11	14	12																	1
1	2	3	4	5		12	8	9*	10	11	14	7†																	2
1	14	3	2	4	6		8		10	12	11		5	7†	9*														3
1		3	2	4	6		8	9	10†	11			5	7†		14	12												4
1		3	2	4	6	14	8		10†	11			5	7		12	9*												5
1		3	2	4	6	14	8	9†	10	11			5	7*		12													6
		3	2		6	12	8	9	10	11			5	7*		4		1											7
		3	2	4	6	14	8*	9	10†	11			5	12		7		1											8
		3	2	4	6	10†	14	12	8	11			5	7				1	9*										9
		2	3		6		8	9	10†	11			5	12		4		1	7*	14									10
		2	3		6		8*	9†	10	11			5	12		4		1	7	14									11
		2	3		6		8	9	10†	11			5	7*		4	14	1	12										12
		2			6		8	9†		11			5	12		4	10	1	7*	14			3						13
		3	2		6		8		10†	11			5	12		4	9	1	7*	14									14
		3	2		6		8		12	11			5			4	9	1	7	10*									15
		3	2*		6	10	8			11			5			4	9	1	12	7									16
		3	2		6	12	8†			11			5			4	9*	1	10	7			14						17
		3	2		6	14	8			11*			5			4†	9	1	12	7			10						18
	2	5			6†	7	8			11						4	9*	1	14	12			3	10					19
	2	5				10*		9	14	11						4	12	1	6	7			3	8†					20
	2	14	5		6	12		9		11						4		1	10	7*			3	8†					21
	2*	3	4						10	14	11		5	12			9†	1	6	7				8					22
		3	2			12			10	11†			5	14		4	9	1	6	7*				8					23
1		3	2	14		10*			7	11			5			4			6	12			8†	9					24
1			2		6*	10	8		7	11			5			4				12			3	9					25
1			2		6	10*	8		7	11			5			4				3				9	12				26
	2	3	4			10	12	8	9	11				14				1	6†	7*				5					27
	2	3			6	10	8			11†		9				4		1	7	14				5*	12				28
	2				6*	10	8					9				4	11			7	12			5	3	1			29
1	2				6	10	8					9*	14			4	11†			7	12		3	5					30
1	2				6*		8	9	10†	11			12			4			7			14	3	5					31
1	2					12	8	9	10	11						4			7				3	5			6*		32
	14	2	5				8		12	10	11					4		1	7				3†				6		33
	14	2	8						12	10	11	9*		7†		4		1		3				5			6		34
1	2		8						10	11		9*	5	7		4	14			12			3			5†	6		35
1	14	2	8						10	11		9*	5			4				7	12		3†				6		36
14	11	25	30	11	24	8	27	24	22	32		8	22	9	1	27	11	21	17	13	1	13	7	11		1	1	5	
4	1		2	10	1	4	3		2	1		9	4	3		4	7	7		1			1	1					
	1			5	3	3	6	12	5		1	2			4		3	1				1							

43

1985-86

1	Aug	10	(h)	Dundee U	W	1-0	McCoist	28,035
2		17	(a)	Hibernian	W	3-1	McCoist, McPherson, Williamson	14,500
3		24	(h)	Hearts	W	3-1	Burns, Williamson 2	35,483
4		31	(a)	Celtic	D	1-1	McCoist	58,365
5	Sep	7	(h)	St. Mirren	W	3-0	Fleck, Cooper, Burns	27,707
6		14	(a)	Clydebank	W	1-0	Williamson	9,980
7		21	(h)	Dundee	L	0-1		23,600
8		28	(h)	Aberdeen	L	0-3		37,599
9	Oct	5	(a)	Motherwell	W	3-0	McCoist 2, McPherson	12,711
10		12	(a)	Dundee U	D	1-1	McCoist	15,821
11		19	(h)	Hibernian	L	1-2	Cooper (pen)	23,478
12		26	(a)	St. Mirren	L	1-2	McCoist	13,911
13	Nov	2	(h)	Clydebank	D	0-0		16,943
14		9	(h)	Celtic	W	3-0	Durrant, Cooper, McMinn	42,045
15		16	(a)	Hearts	L	0-3		23,083
16		23	(a)	Dundee	L	2-3	McCoist 2	10,798
17	Dec	7	(h)	Motherwell	W	1-0	McCoist	12,872
18		14	(h)	Dundee U	D	1-1	McCoist	17,786
19		21	(a)	Hibernian	D	1-1	Cooper	11,000
20		28	(h)	Hearts	L	0-2		33,410
21	Jan	1	(a)	Celtic	L	0-2		49,789
22		4	(h)	Dundee	W	5-0	McCoist 3, Williamson, Fleck	13,954
23		11	(h)	Clydebank	W	4-2	Paterson, McPherson, Williamson, McCoist	12,731
24		18	(h)	St. Mirren	W	2-0	McCoist, McPherson	17,528
25	Feb	1	(h)	Aberdeen	D	1-1	Burns	29,887
26		8	(a)	Motherwell	L	0-1		11,619
27		19	(a)	Aberdeen	L	0-1		18,700
28		22	(a)	Dundee U	D	1-1	McCoist	14,644
29	Mar	1	(h)	Hibernian	W	3-1	McCoist 3 (1 pen)	16,574
30		15	(a)	Dundee	L	1-2	McCoist	10,965
31		22	(h)	Celtic	D	4-4	Fraser 2, McCoist, Fleck	41,006
32		29	(a)	Hearts	L	1-3	McCoist (pen)	24,735
33	Apr	12	(a)	Clydebank	L	1-2	Durrant	7,027
34		19	(a)	St. Mirren	L	1-2	Dawson	9,760
35		26	(a)	Aberdeen	D	1-1	McMinn	17,000
36	May	3	(h)	Motherwell	W	2-0	McPherson, McCoist (pen)	21,500

FINAL LEAGUE POSITION : 5th in Premier Division

Appearances

Sub. Appearances

Goals

44

Walker	Burns	Munro	McPherson	Patterson	Durrant	McCoist	Russell	Williamson	Ferguson D	Cooper	McMinn	MacKinnon	Bell	Fleck	Ferguson I	Dawson	Fraser C	Beattie	Johnstone	Nisbet	Miller	Ferguson E	MacDonald	McCloy	No.
1	2	3	4	5	6	7	8	9*	10†	11	12	14													1
1	2	3	4	5	10	7	8	9*		11†			14	6	12										2
1	2	3	4	5	10*	7	8	9		11			12	6											3
1	2	3	4	5		7	8†	9		11*			10	6	12	14									4
1	2	3	4	5	10†		8	9	14	11	12		6	7*											5
1	2	3	4	5	10		8†	9		11	14	12	6*	7											6
1	2	3	4	5		12		9		11	14	8*	6	7†		10							.		7
1	2	3	4	5	6*	7	8	9†		11	12	14	10												8
1		3	4	10*	7	8	9	12		11			2	6		5									9
1	2*	3	4	10	7	8	9†	12		11			5	14		6									10
1	2	3		10	7	8	12	14		11	6		9†	4*		5									11
1	2†	3		10	7	8	14	11		12	4		9*	6		5									12
1		3	4		7			12	10	11†	14	5	6			2	8		9*						13
1		3	4	10	7	12	9†	8*		11	14	5	6			2									14
1	14	3	4	10	7	8		9*		11	12	5	6†			2									15
1	14	3	4	10*	7	12				11	9	5	6†	8		2									16
1		3	4		8	10	12			11	14	6	7			2	5†		9*						17
1		3	4	10	7	14	8†			11	12	2	6*				5		9						18
1		3	4	5	6	7	8	10		11	12					2			9*						19
1		3	4	5	6	7	8	10	11†	12	14					2			9*						20
1		3	4	5	6	7	8	9	10†	11*	12	14				2									21
1	2	3	8	5	10†	11	14	9		6	7*	12				4									22
1	2	1	5	6*	11	12	9	8		7†	14					4				3					23
1	2	10	5	6	7	12	9†	8*		11						4				3		14			24
1	2	10			8			9*		11	7	6	12			3	5		4						25
1	2	10	5		8			9*		11	7	6	12			3			4						26
1	2	10	5		11†	8	9	12			7	6				3		14	4*						27
1	2	10	5		6*		9	12		11	7					3		8	4						28
1	2	10	5		6		9			11	7	12	14			3		8†	4*						29
1	2	3	4	10	8					11	7		9*	12		6		5							30
1	2†	3	4		6	11	8		14	12	7*	5	9			10									31
1	2	3	4		6	11	14			12	7	5	10†	9*		8									32
1	2	3	5		6	9	12	8	14	7†	4		10*									11			33
	2	12	4	6*	9	14	11	8		7						3	5					10†	1		34
	2	3	5		8	9					7	11	10			4	6						1		35
1	2	3	5		8*	9				11	10	4	7			6					12				36
34	26	28	34	18	30	33	17	20	12	28	15	18	20	9	1	23	7	5	8	4	2		2	2	
	2	1					10	3	7	4	13	6	3	6	3	1	1			1		1			
		3		5	1	2	24		6		4	2		3		1	2								

1986-87

1	Aug	9	(a)	Hibernian	L	1-2	McCoist (pen)	24,576
2		13	(h)	Falkirk	W	1-0	McCoist (pen)	27,362
3		16	(h)	Dundee U	L	2-3	McCoist 2	43,995
4		23	(a)	Hamilton A	W	2-1	Fraser, West	10,000
5		31	(h)	Celtic	W	1-0	Durrant	43,502
6	Sep	6	(a)	Motherwell	W	2-0	Cooper, McPherson	17,013
7		13	(h)	Clydebank	W	4-0	Fleck 3, McMinn	25,866
8		20	(a)	Dundee	L	0-1		17,132
9		27	(h)	Aberdeen	W	2-0	Souness, McCoist	40,155
10	Oct	4	(a)	Hearts	D	1-1	Cooper	28,637
11		8	(a)	St. Mirren	W	1-0	Cooper	16,766
12		11	(h)	Hibernian	W	3-0	McPherson, Fleck, Bell	36,196
13		18	(a)	Falkirk	W	5-1	Fleck 3 (1 pen), Cooper 2 (1 pen)	16,800
14		29	(a)	Dundee U	D	0-0		20,171
15	Nov	1	(a)	Celtic	D	1-1	McCoist	60,000
16		8	(h)	Motherwell	L	0-1		30,966
17		15	(a)	Clydebank	W	4-1	McCoist 2, McPherson, Durrant	9,906
18		19	(h)	Dundee	W	2-1	McCoist, Ferguson	22,992
19		22	(a)	Aberdeen	L	0-1		21,733
20		29	(h)	Hearts	W	3-0	McCoist, Cooper, Durrant	38,733
21	Dec	3	(h)	St. Mirren	W	2-0	McPherson, Ferguson (og)	23,110
22		6	(a)	Hibernian	D	0-0		18,536
23		13	(h)	Falkirk	W	4-0	Butcher 2, Fleck 2	23,177
24		20	(a)	Hamilton A	W	2-0	Fleck, McCoist	10,000
25		27	(h)	Dundee U	W	2-0	McCoist, Fleck	42,165
26	Jan	1	(h)	Celtic	W	2-0	Fleck, McCoist	43,206
27		6	(a)	Motherwell	W	1-0	Roberts	19,658
28		10	(h)	Clydebank	W	5-0	McCoist 2 (1 pen), Fleck	36,397
29		17	(h)	Hamilton A	W	2-0	Durrant, McCoist	43,052
30		24	(h)	Aberdeen	D	0-0		43,211
31	Feb	7	(a)	Hearts	W	5-2	Fleck 2, Roberts, Black (og), McCoist	29,000
32		14	(a)	St. Mirren	W	3-1	McCoist 3 (1 pen)	21,399
33		28	(h)	Hibernian	D	1-1	McPherson	38,630
34	Mar	7	(a)	Falkirk	W	2-1	McCoist 2	17,000
35		14	(h)	Hamilton A	W	2-0	Cooper, McCoist	33,486
36		17	(a)	Dundee	W	4-0	McCoist 2, McPherson, Fleck	18,723
37		21	(a)	Dundee U	W	1-0	McPherson	21,275
38		28	(h)	Motherwell	W	1-0	McCoist	37,305
39	Apr	4	(a)	Celtic	L	1-3	McCoist	60,800
40		14	(h)	Dundee	W	2-0	Cooper, McCoist	42,427
41		18	(a)	Clydebank	W	3-0	McCoist 2 (1 pen), West	9,950
42		25	(h)	Heart	W	3-0	McCoist 3 (1 pen)	43,205
43	May	2	(a)	Aberdeen	D	1-1	Butcher	23,500
44		9	(h)	St. Mirren	W	1-0	Fleck	43,150

FINAL LEAGUE POSITION : 1st in Premier Division

Appearances

Sub. Appearances

Goals

46

Woods	Dawson	Munro	Souness	McPherson	Butcher	Russell	West	McCoist	Durrant	McMinn	Ferguson D	Fleck	Nicholl	Fraser	Cooper	Burns	Nisbet	Walker	MacFarlane	Bell	Paterson	Roberts	Woods	Phillips	
1	2	3	4	5	6	7*	8	9	10†	11	12	14													1
1		3		5	6		8	9	10	11	4		2	7											2
1		3	4	5	6		8	9	10*		12		2	7	11										3
1		3		5	6		8	9	10		4			7	11	2									4
1		3		5	6			9			8	4	2	7	11										5
		3	4	5	6			9	10		8*	12	2	7	11			1							6
		3	4	5	6			9†	10	14	12	8	2	7	11*			1							7
1	6	3		5				9	10		4*	8	2	7	11		12								8
1	12	3	4	5	6			9	10		8†	14	2	7	11*										9
1		3		5	6			9	10			8	2	7*	11				4	12					10
1		3	12	5	6			9	10		7*	8	2		11				4						11
1		3	4†	5	6			9	10		7	8	2		11*				12	14					12
1		3		5	6			9	10		4	8	2		11					7					13
1	5	3			6			9	10	14	4*	8†	2		11				12	7					14
1		3		5	6			9	10	14	4*	8	2	7†	11					12					15
1		3		5	6			9	10		4	8	2	7*	11					12					16
1		3		5	6			9	10		12	8	2	4*	11					7					17
1		3		5	6			9	10		12	8	2	4	11					7*					18
1		3		5	6			9	10		4	12	2	7	11					8*					19
1		3			6		14	9	10†		7	8	2		11	4*				12	5				20
1		3		5	6			9	10		7	8	2		11					4					21
1		3		5	6			9		12	7	8			11	2*				10	4				22
1	2	3		5	6			9	10		4	8		7	11										23
1		3	4	5	6		12	9	10		7*	8			11							2			24
1		3	4	5	6			9	10		7	8			11							2			25
1		3	4	5	6			9	10		7	8			11							2			26
1		3	4	5	6			9	10		7	8			11							2			27
1		3	4	5	6			9	10	12	7	8			11*							2			28
1		3		5	6			9	10		7	8*		4	11							2	12		29
1	10	3	4	5	6			9*			7	8	2		11								12		30
1		3	4	5	6			9	10		7	6			11							2			31
1		3	4	5	6			9	10			8*		7	11							2	12		32
1		3	4	5	6			9	10			8		7	11							2			33
1		3	4	5	6			9	10			8		7	11							2			34
1		3	4	5	6			9	10			8		7	11							2			35
1		3	4	5	6			9	10			8		7	11							2			36
1		3	4	5	6			9	10			8		7	11							2			37
1		3	4	5	6		14	9	10	12		8		7†	11*							2			38
1		3	4	5*	6			9	10		7	8		12	11†							2		14	39
1		3	4*	5	6			9	10		2	8		7	11								12		40
1		3		5	6		14	9	10		2	8†		7*	11						4		12		41
1		3	4	5	6			9	10		2*	8			11					7		12			42
1		3		5	6		14	9†	10			8*		7	11							2	12		43
1		3		5	6			9	10		2	8		7*	11							4	12	14	44
42	6	43	24	42	43	1	4	44	39	9	26	35	34	16	42	3		2	2	7	2	18			
	1		1				5				6	4	5	1			1		2	5		3	6	1	
		1		7	3		2	33	4	1	1	19		1	8					1		2			

47

1987-88

#	Month	Date		Opponent		Score	Scorers	Attendance
1	Aug	8	(h)	Dundee U	D	1-1	McCoist (pen)	39,120
2		12	(a)	Hibernian	L	0-1		22,000
3		15	(a)	Aberdeen	L	0-2		22,500
4		22	(h)	Falkirk	W	4-0	McCoist 3, Falco	32,340
5		29	(a)	Celtic	L	0-1		60,800
6	Sep	5	(h)	Dundee	W	2-1	Fleck, McCoist	38,302
7		12	(h)	Dunfermline A	W	4-0	McCoist 3, Souness	39,749
8		19	(a)	Motherwell	W	1-0	Philliben (og)	19,480
9		26	(h)	Morton	W	7-0	McCoist 3 (1 pen), Falco 3, Fleck	35,843
10	Oct	3	(a)	Hearts	D	0-0		29,000
11		6	(h)	St. Mirren	W	3-1	Falco, Butcher, Souness	39,298
12		10	(a)	Dundee U	L	0-1		18,214
13		17	(h)	Celtic	D	2-2	McCoist, Gough	44,000
14		28	(a)	Dunferline A	W	4-0	Durrant 2, McCall, McCoist (pen)	18,000
15		31	(h)	Motherwell	W	1-0	McCoist	36,583
16	Nov	7	(h)	Hibernian	W	1-0	Fleck	37,517
17		14	(a)	St. Mirren	D	2-2	McCoist 2	20,469
18		17	(h)	Aberdeen	L	0-1		41,371
19		21	(a)	Falkirk	W	1-0	Fleck	17,500
20		24	(a)	Morton	W	3-0	Ferguson D, Fleck, McCoist	15,500
21		28	(h)	Hearts	W	3-2	Fleck, Levein (og), Durrant	43,557
22	Dec	5	(h)	Dundee U	W	1-0	McCoist (pen)	41,159
23		12	(a)	Hibernian	W	2-0	Gough, Fleck	19,000
24		15	(h)	Dunfermline A	D	2-2	Ferguson D, McCoist	31,687
25		19	(a)	Motherwell	W	2-0	Philliben (og), McCoist (pen)	15,346
26		26	(h)	Dundee	W	2-0	McCoist 2 (1 pen)	40,938
27	Jan	2	(a)	Celtic	L	0-2		60,800
28		6	(a)	Dundee	W	1-0	McCoist	17,450
29		9	(h)	Morton	W	5-0	McCoist 3, Durrant 2	38,349
30		16	(a)	Hearts	D	1-1	Durrant (pen)	28,967
31		23	(h)	Falkirk	W	3-1	Bertram, Brown, Durrant (pen)	41,088
32	Feb	6	(a)	Aberdeen	W	2-1	McCoist, Gough	22,500
33		13	(h)	St. Mirren	W	4-0	Cooper, Walters, Wilkins, Gough	41,664
34		27	(a)	Dundee U	D	1-1	Walters	20,846
35	Mar	5	(a)	Dunfermline A	W	3-0	McCoist (pen), Walters, Gough	19,017
36		12	(h)	Motherwell	W	1-0	Durrant	39,650
37		20	(h)	Celtic	L	1-2	Bertram	43,650
38		26	(a)	Dundee	W	3-2	Roberts, Walters, Durrant (pen)	14,879
39	Apr	2	(h)	Hearts	L	1-2	Bartram	41,125
40		9	(a)	Morton	L	2-3	Ferguson I, Durrant	11,000
41		16	(h)	Hibernian	D	1-1	Ferguson D	32,218
42		23	(a)	St. Mirren	W	3-0	Walters, Brown, McCoist	13,809
43		30	(h)	Aberdeen	L	0-1		36,010
44	May	7	(a)	Falkirk	W	5-0	Walters 2, McCoist 2 (1 pen), Ferguson D	11,500

FINAL LEAGUE POSITION : 3rd in Premier Division

Appearances

Sub. Appearances

Goals

Woods	Nicholl	Munro	Ferguson D	McGregor	Cohen	Kirkwood	Falco	McCoist	Phillips	Cooper	Durrant	Fleck	MacFarlane	Nisbet	West	Roberts	Butcher	Souness	McCall	Francis	Gough	Wilkins	Walters	Walker	Brown	Bertram	Ferguson	McSwegan	
1	2	3	4	5	6	7†	8	9	10*	11	12	14																	1
1		3		5	6†	4	8	9	11		10	7*	2	12	14														2
1	2	3*		5		7†	12	9	11		10	14				4	6	8											3
1	2		7†	12			8	9	3	11	10	14				4*	6	5											4
1	2	3	7	6			8	9		11*	10					4		5	12										5
1	2			6				9	3	11	7	8				4		5	10										6
1	2		5					9†	3	14	10*	8				4	6	12	7	11									7
1	2			12				9	3	14	11*	8				4	6	5	10†	7									8
1	2		5	12			8	9	3		11†	14				4*	6		10	7									9
1	2	5	4				8†	9	3	7	11	14					6		10*	12									10
1	2		4				8	9	3*	11	10						6	5	12	7									11
1	11	3	7	5*		8†		9				14				4	6		10	12	2								12
1		5	11	12		8*		9	3	14	10					4	6		7†		2								13
1	2	5		14		12		9	3	11	7*	8					6†		10		4								14
1	2	11†		3		14		9		12	10	8*				4		5		7	6								15
1	2	7	3					9		11	10	8				4		5*		12	6								16
1	2		5					9	3	11	7	8				4			10*	12	6								17
1	12	5	2				14	9		11	10	8				4	6*			7†	3								18
1		7	5					9	3	11	10	8		2		4					6								19
1		7	5†				14	9	3	11*	10	8		2		4				12	6								20
1		7	14					9	3	11*	10	8		2		4				12	6	5†							21
1		11						9	3	12	10	8		2		4				7*	6	5							22
1		11	3					9		7	10	8		2		4					6	5							23
1		11*	3					9		7	10	8		2		4			12		6	5							24
1	3	11						9		7	10			2		4		8			6	5							25
1	3	11						9		7*	10			2		4		8	12		6	5							26
1†	3		14					9		11*	10			2		4		8	12		6	5	7						27
	3		7					9			10			2		4		8			6	5	11	1					28
	2†	3	7*	8				9			10		14			4					6	5	11	1					29
	3		14					9			10*			2		4		7			6	5	11	1	8†				30
		7						9		12	10			2		4*					6	5	11	1	8	3			31
1		7†	8*					9		14	10			2		4		12				5	11		6	3			32
1	12	8†								7	10*			2		4		9	14		6	5	11			3			33
1	2	8								12	10			9*		4					6	5	11			3	7		34
1		8						9*		12	10			2		4					6	5	11			3	7		35
1		7						9†		14	10			2		4		12			6	5	11		3*	8			36
1		7						9			10			2		4					6	5	11			3	8		37
1		7						9*		12	10			2		4					6	5	11			3	8		38
1		7									10			2		4					6	5	11		9	3	8		39
1		12						9†	8		10			2		4*		14				5	11		6	3	7		40
	2	3	7†							12	10					4						5	11	1	6*	8	9	14	41
1	2	3	7					9		11						4					6	5	8		10				42
1	2	3	7					9		11				12		4					6	5	8		10*				43
1	2	3	7			12		9	10			8*				4						5	11		6				44
39	21	16	31	20	4	3	9	40	19	21	39	15	1	22		37	11	14	8	8	31	24	18	5	9	11	8		
	1	1	1	5	3	1	5			12	1	6		3	1			4	4	10								1	
		4			5	31		1	10	7			1	1	2	1		5	1	7			2	3	1				

49

1988-89

1	Aug	13	(a)	Hamilton A	W	2-0	Stevens, McCoist	10,500
2		20	(h)	Hibernian	D	0-0		41,955
3		27	(h)	Celtic	W	5-1	McCoist, Wilkins, Drinkell 2, Walters	42,858
4	Sep	3	(a)	Motherwell	W	2-0	Drinkell, Durrant	20,112
5		17	(a)	Hearts	W	2-1	Durrant (pen), Nisbet	25,401
6		24	(h)	St. Mirren	W	2-1	Cooper D (pen), Walters	35,523
7		27	(a)	Dundee U	W	1-0	Ferguson I	20,071
8	Oct	1	(h)	Dundee	W	2-0	Drinkell, Walters	40,768
9		8	(a)	Aberdeen	L	1-2	Cooper N	22,370
10		12	(a)	Hibernian	W	1-0	McCoist	25,000
11		29	(a)	St. Mirren	D	1-1	Gray	20,490
12	Nov	1	(h)	Hearts	W	3-0	Gough, Walters (pen), Gray	36,505
13		5	(h)	Motherwell	W	2-1	Brown, Drinkell	35,060
14		12	(a)	Celtic	L	1-3	Walters (pen)	60,113
15		16	(h)	Hamilton A	W	3-1	Gray, Ferguson I, Drinkell	33,864
16		19	(a)	Dundee	D	0-0		16,514
17		26	(h)	Aberdeen	W	1-0	Gough	42,239
18	Dec	3	(h)	Dundee U	L	0-1		39,123
19		10	(a)	Hearts	L	0-2		26,424
20		17	(h)	Hibernian	W	1-0	McCall	36,472
21		31	(a)	Hamilton A	W	1-0	Ferguson D	10,500
22	Jan	3	(h)	Celtic	W	4-1	Butcher, Walters 2 (1 pen), Gough	42,515
23		7	(a)	Motherwell	L	1-2	Drinkell	19,275
24		14	(a)	Aberdeen	W	2-1	Ferguson D, Munro	22,000
25		21	(h)	Dundee	W	3-1	Ferguson I, Butcher, McCoist	43,202
26	Feb	11	(a)	Dundee U	D	1-1	Munro	22,019
27		25	(h)	St. Mirren	W	3-1	Ferguson I, McCoist, Walters	39,021
28	Mar	11	(h)	Hamilton A	W	3-0	Ferguson I, Sterland, Gough	24,112
29		25	(a)	Hibernian	W	1-0	Drinkell	22,000
30	Apr	1	(a)	Celtic	W	2-1	Drinkell, McCoist	60,800
31		8	(h)	Motherwell	W	1-0	McCoist	37,782
32		22	(a)	St. Mirren	W	2-0	Ferguson I, McCoist	22,096
33		29	(h)	Hearts	W	4-0	Sterland 2, Drinkell 2	42,856
34	May	2	(h)	Dundee U	W	2-0	Drinkell, McCoist	39,058
35		6	(a)	Dundee	W	2-1	Gray 2	14,889
36		13	(h)	Aberdeen	L	0-3		42,480

FINAL LEAGUE POSITION : 1st in Premier Division

Appearances

Sub. Appearances

Goals

Woods	Stevens	Munro	Gough	Wilkins	Butcher	Drinkell	Brown	McCoist	Durrant	Walters	Ferguson D	Cooper D	Souness	Ferguson I	Nisbet	Gray	Cooper N	Walker	MacDonald	McCall	McSwegan	Cowan	Sterland	Nicholl	Kirkwood	Robertson	
1	2	3	4	5	6	7	8*	9†	10	11	12	14															1
1	2		4	5*	6	7	3	9	10†	11	8	14	12														2
1	2		4	5	6	7	3	9	10*	11†		14	12	8													3
1	2		4	5	6	7	3		10	11			9	8													4
1	2		4	5*	6	7†	3		10	11			9	12	8	14											5
1	2		4	5	6		3*		10	11			9	12	8	7†	14										6
1	2	3	4	5	6			9	10	11		12		8		7*											7
1	2	3	4	5	6	7†	10	9*		11		12		8		14											8
1	2	12	4		6	7	3	9	10*	11†		14	8		5												9
1	2		4	5	6	7	3	9		11*		12	8			10											10
1	2	3†	4	5	6	7	11	9*			12		8	14		10											11
1	2		4	5	6	7	3			11			8	9*		12	10										12
1	2		4	5	6	7	3			11	12		8	9†		14	10*										13
1	2		4	5	6	7	3			11		9	8	12			10*										14
	2	3	4	5	6	7				11*		14	8	12	9	10†	1										15
	2	3	4	5	6	7	10			11			8			9	1										16
	2		4	5	6	7	3			11*		9	8			10	1		12								17
	2		4	5	6	7	3					9	8	12		10	1		11*								18
	2		4	5	6	7	3			11		9	8	12			1		10*								19
	2	3	4	5	6	7	9*			11		12	8				1			10							20
	2	3	4	5	6	7						12	8	9†		11*	1			10	14						21
	2	3	4	5*	6	7	10†			11		9	8	12			1			14							22
	2	3	4	5	6	7	10*			11		9	8				1			12							23
	2	3	4	5*	6	7	10			11		9	8	12			1										24
	2	3†		5*	6	7	10	14		11		9	8	12			1						4				25
	2	3	4	5*	6	7	10			11		9	8	12			1										26
1	2	3	4	5*	6			9	10	11†		14	8			12	7										27
1	2		4		6	7		9	10	11			8							3	5						28
1	2	3	4	12	6	7		9	10	11*			8								5						29
1	2	3	4	5	6	7	10*	9		11†		14	8								12						30
1	2	3	4	5	6	7	10*	9		11			12								8						31
1	2		4	5*	6	7	3	9	10	11		14		8†							12						32
1	2	3	4	5*	6	7	9†	10		11		14									12		8				33
1	2	3†	4		6	7	9			11*		14		12							10		8	5			34
1	2	3*	4		6		9			11						7			14		10		8	5†	12		35
1		3	4		6	7	10	9†		11		12	8			14							2			5*	36
24	35	21	35	30	34	32	29	18	8	30	12	9	30	5	3	11	12	2	2	3	7	1	2	1			
		1	1				1			1			1	4	14	6	2	10	3	1	3	1	1	2		1	
	1	2	4	1	2	12	1	9	2	8	2	1		6	1	5	1			1	3						

51

1989-90

1	Aug	12	(h)	St. Mirren	L	0-1		39,951
2		19	(a)	Hibernian	L	0-2		21,500
3		26	(a)	Celtic	D	1-1	Butcher	50,000
4	Sep	9	(h)	Aberdeen	W	1-0	Johnston	40,283
5		16	(h)	Dundee	D	2-2	McCoist 2	35,836
6		23	(a)	Dunfermline A	D	1-1	McCoist	17,765
7		30	(h)	Hearts	W	1-0	Johnston	39,554
8	Oct	3	(a)	Motherwell	L	0-1		17,667
9		14	(h)	Dundee U	W	2-1	Johnston, McCoist	36,062
10		25	(a)	St. Mirren	W	2-0	McCoist, Johnston	15,130
11		28	(h)	Hibernian	W	3-0	McCoist 2, Johnston (pen)	35,260
12	Nov	4	(h)	Celtic	W	1-0	Johnston	41,598
13		18	(a)	Dundee	W	2-0	Walters, Johnston	14,536
14		22	(a)	Aberdeen	L	0-1		23,000
15		25	(h)	Dunfermline A	W	3-0	Johnston, Butcher, McCoist	39,121
16	Dec	2	(a)	Hearts	W	2-1	Walters, Steven	24,771
17		9	(h)	Motherwell	W	3-0	Butcher, McCoist, Brown	33,549
18		16	(a)	Dundee U	D	1-1	Johnston	15,947
19		23	(h)	St. Mirren	W	1-0	Dodds	31,797
20		30	(a)	Hibernian	D	0-0		17,000
21	Jan	2	(a)	Celtic	W	1-0	Spackman	54,000
22		6	(h)	Aberdeen	W	2-0	Walters, McCoist	41,351
23		13	(h)	Dundee	W	3-0	McCoist, Dodds, Johnston	36,993
24		27	(a)	Dunfermline A	W	1-0	Stevens	17,350
25	Feb	3	(h)	Dundee U	W	3-1	Walters, McCoist, Johnston	39,058
26		10	(a)	Motherwell	D	1-1	Johnston	17,647
27		17	(h)	Hearts	D	0-0		41,884
28	Mar	3	(a)	Dundee	D	2-2	Johnston, Dodds	12,743
29		17	(a)	St. Mirren	D	0-0		15,122
30		24	(h)	Hibernian	L	0-1		37,542
31	Apr	1	(h)	Celtic	W	3-0	Walters (pen), Johnston, McCoist (pen)	41,926
32		8	(a)	Aberdeen	D	0-0		23,000
33		14	(h)	Motherwell	W	2-1	Steven, Johnston	39,305
34		21	(a)	Dundee U	W	1-0	Steven	15,995
35		28	(h)	Dunfermline A	W	2-0	McCoist, Dodds	40,769
36	May	5	(a)	Hearts	D	1-1	Munro	20,283

FINAL LEAGUE POSITION : 1st in Premier Division

Appearances

Sub. Appearances

Goals

Woods	Stevens	Munro	Gough	Wilkins	Butcher	Steven	Ferguson I	McCoist	Johnston	Walters	Drinkell	Ferguson D	Ginzburg	Nisbet	Brown	Cowan	Dodds	Cooper N	McCall	Spackman	Vinnicombe	Robertson	Souness	
1*	2	3	4	5	6	7	8	9†	10	11	14	12												1
	2	3	4	5	6	7	8	9	10	11*	12		1		11									2
	2	3	4	5	6	7	8	12	10	9*			1		11									3
1				5	6	7	8	14	10†	11	9			12	4*									4
1	2	3	5*		6	7	12	9	10	11		8		4										5
1	2	3	4	5	6	7	12	9	10	11		8*												6
	2	3	4	5	6	7	8†	9	10	11*			1			12	14							7
	2	3	4	5	6	7		9	10				1				8	11*	12					8
1	2	3	4	5	6	7		9	10	11*							12	8†	14					9
1	2	3	4	5	6	7	8	9	10									11						10
1	2	3	4*	5	6	7	8	9	10								14	12	11†					11
1	2	3		5	6	7	8	9	10	11					4									12
1	2†	3		5	6	7	8	9	10	11*				14	4			12						13
1	2	3		5	6	7	8	9	10	11					4									14
1	2	3		5	6	7	8	9	10	11					4									15
1	2	3			6	7	8	9	10	11					4					5				16
1	2	3*	4		6	7	8	9	10						11					5	12			17
1	2	3	4		6	7	8	9	10						11					5				18
1	2	3†	4		6	7*	8	9	10						11			12		5	14			19
1	2	3	4		6			9	10	7					11	8				5				20
1	2	3*	4		6	7		9	10	8					11					5	12			21
1	2	3	4		6	7		9	10	8*					11					5	12			22
1	2	3	4		6	7		9*	10	8					11			12		5				23
1	2	3	4			7		9	10	8				6	11					5				24
1	2	3	4			7		9	10	8*					11					5	6	12		25
1	2	3			6	7	4*	9	10	8					11			12		5				26
1	2	3			6	7	4	9	10	8					11					5				27
1	2	3			6	7	8		10					4*	11		9			5	12			28
1	2	3	4		6	7	8		10					9	11*		12			5				29
1	2	3	4		6	7	12	9	10	8					11*					5				30
1	2	3	4		6	7*	8	9	10	11					12					5				31
1	2†	3	4		6	7	8*	9	10	11					14			12		5				32
1		3	4		6	7		9	10	11		14		12	2*	8†				5				33
1	2	3	4		6	7		9	10	11		8*			12					5				34
1	2	3†	4		6	7		9*	10	11					8			12		5		14		35
1	2	3	4		6			9*	10	11					8†	7	14			5	12			36
32	35	36	26	15	34	34	21	32	36	27	2	3	4	4	24	1	4	2	2	21	1			
							3	2				2	2	3	3	2	10	1	2		6	1	1	
	1	1			3	3		14	15	5					1		4			1				

1990-91

1	Aug	25	(h)	Dunfermline A	W	3-1	Hateley, Johnston, Walters (pen)	39,951
2	Sep	1	(a)	Hibernian	D	0-0		17,500
3		8	(a)	Hearts	W	3-1	Huistra, McCoist 2	22,101
4		15	(h)	Celtic	D	1-1	Hurlock	38,543
5		22	(a)	Dundee U	L	1-2	Johnston	16,270
6		29	(h)	Motherwell	W	1-0	Brown	34,863
7	Oct	6	(a)	Aberdeen	D	0-0		24,000
8		13	(h)	St. Mirren	W	5-0	McCoist 2 (1 pen), Walters 2, Johnston	38,031
9		20	(a)	St. Johnstone	D	0-0		10,504
10	Nov	3	(h)	Hibernian	W	4-0	Hateley 2, Walters, Steven	33,725
11		10	(h)	Dundee U	L	1-2	McCoist	36,995
12		17	(a)	Motherwell	W	4-2	Walters, Johnston, Stevens 2	16,457
13		20	(a)	Dunfermline A	W	1-0	Hateley	14,480
14		25	(a)	Celtic	W	2-1	Johnston, McCoist	52,265
15	Dec	1	(h)	Hearts	W	4-0	Johnston, Hurlock, McCoist, Walters (pen)	37,623
16		8	(h)	St. Johnstone	W	4-1	Walters 2, Johnston (pen), Stevens	34,610
17		15	(a)	St. Mirren	W	3-0	Walters, Johnston, Hateley	15,197
18		22	(h)	Aberdeen	D	2-2	McCoist 2	37,998
19		29	(a)	Dundee U	W	2-1	Johnston, Walters	17,564
20	Jan	2	(h)	Celtic	W	2-0	Walters, Hateley	38,398
21		5	(a)	Hearts	W	1-0	Hateley	20,956
22		12	(h)	Dunfermline A	W	2-0	Huistra, Johnston	35,120
23		19	(a)	Hibernian	W	2-0	Johnston, Vinnicombe	15,000
24	Feb	9	(h)	St. Mirren	W	1-0	McCoist	31,769
25		16	(h)	Motherwell	W	2-0	McCoist, Hateley	32,192
26		26	(a)	St. Johnstone	D	1-1	Huistra	10,721
27	Mar	2	(a)	Aberdeen	L	0-1		22,500
28		9	(h)	Hearts	W	2-1	Steven, Walters	36,128
29		24	(a)	Celtic	L	0-3		52,000
30		30	(a)	Dunfermline A	W	1-0	Stevens	14,256
31	Apr	6	(h)	Hibernian	D	0-0		35,507
32		13	(h)	St. Johnstone	W	3-0	Durrant, Spencer, Huistra	35,930
33		20	(a)	St. Mirren	W	1-0	Robertson	18,473
34		24	(h)	Dundee U	W	1-0	Ferguson I	32,397
35	May	4	(a)	Motherwell	L	0-3		17,672
36		11	(h)	Aberdeen	W	2-0	Hateley 2	37,652

FINAL LEAGUE POSITION : 1st in Premier Division

Appearances

Sub. Appearances

Goals

Woods	Stevens	Brown	Gough	Spackman	Butcher	Steven	Ferguson I	Hateley	Johnston	Walters	McCoist	Huistra	Hurlock	Munro	Kuznetsov	Nisbet	Robertson	McSwegan	Vinnicombe	Dodds	Spencer	Reid	Durrant	Cowan	
1	2	3	4	5	6	7	8†	9	10	11*	12	14													1
1	2	3	4	5	6	7	8	9*	10		12		11												2
1	2		4	5	6	7		9	10	12	8	11*	3												3
1	2	12	4	5	6	7		9†	10	14	8	11*	3												4
1	2	12	4	5	6	7		9†	10	14	8	11*	3												5
1	2	6	4	5		7		12	10	8	9*	11		3											6
1	2	6	4	5		7		12	10	11*	9		8	3											7
1	2		4	5		7			10	11	9	12	8	3*	6										8
1	2		4	5		7		14	10	11	9†	12	8	3	6*										9
1	2		4	5		7*	12		10	11†	9	14	8	3		6									10
1	2	6		5		7*			10	11	9		8	3†		4	12	14							11
1	2	6		5				9	10	11*	12					4	8		3	7					12
1	2	6		5				8	10		9		7			4			3	11					13
1	2	6*		5				9	10†	11	14	12	7	3		4	8								14
1	2	6		5				9	10*	11	12		7	3		4	8								15
1	2	6		5		7*		9	10	11†	14	12	8	3		4									16
1	2	6	4	5		7		9	10	11*	12		8	3											17
1	2	6	4			7†		9	10	11	14	12	8	3			5*								18
1	2	6	4	5				9	10†	11	14	12		3			8		7*						19
1	2	6	4	5				9	10	7		11*	8	3					12						20
1	2	6	4	5				9	10	7		11*	8	3					12						21
1	2	6*	4	5				9	10	7		11	8						12		3				22
1	2		4	5				9	10	7*	14	11	8†				6				3		12		23
1	2	6	4	5		7		8	9	11*							12			10	3				24
1	2	6*	4	5		7		9	8	11	10	12				3									25
1	2	6	4	5		7		9		14	10†	12	11			3*									26
1	2	5	6	4		7		9	10	11*	12		8			3									27
1	2		4	5		7	6*	9		11	10	12	8			3									28
1	2		4	5		8*		10			9				6		12			7	11		3		29
1	2		4	5		8		9	10*	11†	14		7						3		12	6			30
1	2		4	5				9	8	11			7					3*		10	12	6			31
1	2		4	5		8		9			12		7				3	14	11†	10*		6			32
1	2	6		5		8		9			12		7	4			14	11*	3		10†				33
1	2	6	4	5		8		9	10	7*		12					11							3	34
1	2†	6		5		8*		9	10	11	12		7	4			14							3	35
1	2	6†		5		8		9	10	11	14		7	4								12		3*	36
36	36	25	26	35	5	19	10	30	29	26	15	10	29	14	2	15	7	1	10	3	3	3	3	4	
	2					1	3		4	11	17						8	2			2		1	1	
	4	1			2	1		10	11	12	11	4	2			1			1		1		1	1	

55

1991-92

1	Aug	10	(h)	St. Johnstone	W	6-0	Johnston 2 (2 pens), Hateley 3, Ferguson	35,104
2		13	(h)	Motherwell	W	2-0	Maaskant (og), Steven	35,321
3		17	(a)	Hearts	L	0-1		22,534
4		24	(h)	Dunfermline A	W	4-0	Huistra, Johnston, Spencer, McCoist	35,559
5		31	(a)	Celtic	W	2-0	Hateley 2	50,756
6	Sep	7	(a)	Falkirk	W	2-0	Nisbet, Huistra	12,848
7		14	(h)	Dundee U	D	1-1	McCoist	36,347
8		21	(a)	St. Mirren	W	2-1	Huistra, Nisbet	14,503
9		28	(h)	Aberdeen	L	0-2		36,330
10	Oct	5	(a)	Airdrieonians	W	4-0	Nisbet, Johnston, McCoist 2	11,101
11		8	(h)	Hibernian	W	4-2	McCoist 2, Tortolano (og), Huistra	35,364
12		12	(a)	St. Johnstone	W	3-2	McCoist 2, Nisbet	10,322
13		19	(h)	Hearts	W	2-0	McCoist, Mikhailichenko	36,481
14		26	(h)	Falkirk	D	1-1	Johnston	36,441
15		29	(a)	Dundee U	L	2-3	McCoist 2 (1 pen)	15,041
16	Nov	2	(h)	Celtic	D	1-1	McCoist	37,387
17		9	(a)	Dunfermline A	W	5-0	Gough, Gordon 2, Hateley, McCoist	13,351
18		16	(h)	Airdrieonians	W	4-0	Robertson D, Hateley 2, McCoist	36,934
19		19	(a)	Hibernian	W	3-0	McCoist 2, Hateley	16,833
20		23	(h)	St. Mirren	L	0-1		36,272
21		30	(a)	Motherwell	W	2-0	Gordon, Gough	15,350
22	Dec	4	(a)	Aberdeen	W	3-2	Hateley 2, McCoist	20,081
23		7	(h)	St. Johnstone	W	3-1	Mikhailichenko, Brown, Hateley	35,784
24		14	(a)	Falkirk	W	3-1	McCoist, Hateley, McCall	11,801
25		21	(h)	Dundee U	W	2-0	McCoist 2	41,448
26		28	(h)	Dunfermline A	W	2-1	Stevens, Gordon	41,328
27	Jan	1	(a)	Celtic	W	3-1	McCoist, Hateley (pen), Brown	51,789
28		4	(a)	Airdrieonians	D	0-0		12,276
29		11	(h)	Hibernian	W	2-0	Gordon, McCoist	40,616
30		18	(h)	Motherwell	W	2-0	McCoist, Mikhailichenko	38,127
31	Feb	1	(a)	Hearts	W	1-0	McCoist	24,356
32		8	(a)	St. Mirren	W	2-1	McCoist, Mikhailichenko	16,521
33		25	(h)	Aberdeen	D	0-0		38,513
34		29	(a)	Airdrieonians	W	5-0	Brown, Hateley 3 (2 pens), Rideout	40,568
35	Mar	10	(a)	Hibernian	W	3-1	McCoist, Hateley 2	13,387
36		14	(a)	Dunfermline A	W	3-1	Mikhailichenko 2, Nisbet	12,274
37		21	(h)	Celtic	L	0-2		42,160
38		28	(a)	St. Johnstone	W	2-1	Hateley 2	9,697
39	Apr	7	(h)	Falkirk	W	4-1	McCoist 3, Mikhailichenko	36,832
40		11	(a)	Dundee U	W	2-1	Mikhailichenko, Brown	11,713
41		18	(h)	St. Mirren	W	4-0	McCoist 2, Stevens, Huistra	40,362
42		23	(a)	Motherwell	W	2-1	Mikhailichenko 2	12,515
43		28	(h)	Hearts	D	1-1	McCoist	36,129
44	May	2	(a)	Aberdeen	W	2-0	McCoist 2	16,580

FINAL LEAGUE POSITION : 1st in Premier Division

Appearances

Sub. Appearances

Goals

Appearances / substitutes grid (shirt numbers worn; * and † denote substitutions):

Goram	Stevens	Robertson D	Gough	Spackman	Nisbet	Steven	Ferguson	Hateley	Johnston	Huistra	Robertson A	Spencer	McCall	Durrant	McCoist	Mikhailichenko	Kuznetsov	Brown	Vinnicombe	McSwegan	McGregor	Morrow	Gordon	Rideout	Pressley	Robertson L	
1	2	3	4	5	6	7	8*	9	10	11	12																1
1	2	3	4	5	6	7	8	9	10	11																	2
1	2	3	4	5	6		8	9	10	11†			14	7													3
1	2	3	4	5	6		12		9*	11			8	7	10†	14											4
1	2	3	4	5	6		8	9	10	11			7														5
1	2	3	4	5	6		8	9		11	12		7		10*												6
1	2	3		5	6		8	9		11	12		7		10*	4											7
1	2	3	4	5	6			9	10	11			7	8													8
1	2	3		5	6			9*	10	14	8		12	7		11†	4										9
1	2	3		5	6				10	11*	12		8		9	7	4										10
1	2	3		5	6				10	11	7*	14	8		9		4†	12									11
1	2	3		5	6					11†		8	10		9	14	4	7									12
1	2	3	4	5	6				10				8		9	11							7				13
1	2	3	4	5	6		12		10	14			8		9	11*							7†				14
1	2	3		5	6		7†		10	12	11*		8		9	14	4										15
1	2	3		5	6		8†		10	11			7		9	14											16
1	2	3	4	5	6†				10	11			8		9		14						7				17
1	2	3	4	5					10	11			8		9†		6		14				7				18
1	2	3	4	5					10	11			8		9		6						7				19
1	2	3	4	5					10	11†			8		9		6		14				7				20
1	2*	3	4	5					10				8		9	11	6	12					7				21
1	2	3	4	5					10				8		9	11*	6	12					7				22
1	2	3	4	5					10			14	8		9	11*	6	12					7†				23
1	2	3	4	5					10				8		9	11	6						7				24
1	2	3	4	5					10				8		9	11	6*	12					7†				25
1	2*	3	4				5					10	8		9	11	6	12					7				26
1	2	3	4	5					10			14	8*		9	11†	6	12					7				27
1	2	3	4	5					10						9	11	6	8					7				28
1	2	3	4	5									8		9	11	6						7	10			29
1	2	3	4	5			12						8		9	11	6						7	10*			30
1	2	3	4	5									8		10	11	6		14				7†	9			31
1	2	3	4	5									8		9	11	6						7	10			32
1	2	3	4	5			8	10		11			14	9			6						7†				33
1	2	3	4	5†			8	10*		11			14	9			6						7	12			34
1	2	3		5	4		12	10		11			8		9		6						7*				35
1	2	3		5	4		12	10		11			8*	9	7		6										36
1	2	3		5	4		7†	10		12			8		9	11*	14	6									37
1	2	3	4	5					10	11†		7	8*	9	14		6							12			38
1	2		4	5						11			8	10*	9	14	3	6					7†	12			39
1	2	3	4	5					12				8	10*	9†	11		6					7	14			40
1	2		4	5					14				8	10	9	11		6	3				7†				41
1	2*	3		5					7	8			10		9	11	4							6	12		42
1		3		5					10	11*	14		8	12	9		2	6†						4		7	43
1	2	3	4						10				8	6	9	11							7	5			44
44	43	42	33	42	20	2	12	29	10	25	3	4	35	9	37	24	16	18	1		1	3	23	7		1	
	4	1	1		7	3	4	1	4	1		4	1	3	2	7	1	4		1	4			4	1		
	2	1	2		5	1	1	21	5	5		1	1		34	10		4					5	1			

57

1992-93

1	Aug	1	(h)	St. Johnstone	W	1-0	McCoist	38,036
2		4	(h)	Airdrieonians	W	2-0	Gordon, Hateley	36,613
3		8	(a)	Hibernian	D	0-0		17,237
4		15	(a)	Dundee	L	3-4	McCoist 2, Ferguson	12,801
5		22	(h)	Celtic	D	1-1	Durrant	43,239
6		29	(h)	Aberdeen	W	3-1	Durrant, McCoist, Mikhailichenko	41,636
7	Sep	2	(a)	Motherwell	W	4-1	Brown, McCoist 3	10,074
8		12	(a)	Partick T	W	4-1	McPherson, McCall, Gough, Hateley	18,752
9		19	(h)	Hearts	W	2-0	McCall, McCoist	41,888
10		26	(a)	Dundee U	W	4-0	Steven, Huistra 2, McCoist	13,759
11	Oct	3	(h)	Falkirk	W	4-0	McCoist 4	40,691
12		7	(a)	St. Johnstone	W	5-1	Hateley 2, McCoist 2 (1 pen), Ferguson	9,532
13		17	(h)	Hibernian	W	1-0	McCoist	40,978
14		31	(h)	Motherwell	W	4-2	McCoist 3 (1 pen), Brown	38,719
15	Nov	7	(a)	Celtic	W	1-0	Durrant	51,950
16		11	(h)	Dundee	W	3-1	McCoist 2, Hateley	37,255
17		21	(a)	Hearts	D	1-1	McCoist	20,831
18		28	(h)	Partick T	W	3-0	Steven, McSwegan, McPherson	40,939
19	Dec	1	(a)	Aidrieonians	D	1-1	Brown	9,251
20		12	(a)	Falkirk	W	2-1	Hateley, McCoist	11,585
21		19	(h)	St. Johnstone	W	2-0	Gough, Robertson D	37,369
22		26	(a)	Dundee	W	3-1	McCoist, Hateley 2	13,778
23	Jan	2	(h)	Celtic	W	1-0	Steven	46,039
24		5	(h)	Dundee U	W	3-2	Hateley, McCall, McCoist	40,239
25		20	(h)	Hibernian	W	4-3	Mikhailichenko 2, Steven, McCoist	17,447
26	Feb	2	(a)	Aberdeen	W	1-0	Hateley	15,055
27		9	(h)	Falkirk	W	5-0	Huistra, Hateley 2, Steven, Robertson D	37,780
28		13	(h)	Airdrieonians	D	2-2	McCoist 2	39,816
29		20	(a)	Dundee U	D	0-0		13,443
30		23	(a)	Motherwell	W	4-0	McCoist, Hateley 2, Mikhailichenko	14,006
31		27	(h)	Hearts	W	2-1	McCoist, Robertson D	42,128
32	Mar	10	(a)	St. Johnstone	D	1-1	McCoist	9,258
33		13	(h)	Hibernian	W	3-0	Hagen, Hateley, McCoist	41,076
34		20	(a)	Celtic	L	1-2	Hateley	52,779
35		27	(h)	Dundee	W	3-0	McCall, McCoist, Ferguson	40,297
36		30	(h)	Aberdeen	W	2-0	Ferguson, McCoist	44,570
37	Apr	10	(h)	Motherwell	W	1-0	Brown	41,353
38		14	(a)	Hearts	W	3-2	McCall, Hateley 2	14,622
39		17	(h)	Partick T	W	3-1	McSwegan 2, Hagen	42,636
40	May	1	(a)	Airdrieonians	W	1-0	McSwegan	12,514
41		4	(a)	Partick T	L	0-3		9,303
42		8	(h)	Dundee U	W	1-0	Huistra	42,917
43		12	(a)	Aberdeen	L	0-1		13,079
44		15	(a)	Falkirk	W	2-1	Mikhailichenko, Hateley	9,288

FINAL LEAGUE POSITION : 1st in Premier Division

Appearances

Sub. Appearances

Goals

58

Goram	Nisbet	Robertson D	Gough	McPherson	Brown	Durrant	McCall	McCoist	Hateley	Huistra	Rideout	Kuznetsov	Gordon	Mikhailichenko	Steven	Maxwell	Ferguson	Spackman	McSwegan	Hagen	Robertson A	Stevens	Pressley	Murray	Watson	Reid	Robertson L	
1	2	3	4	5†	6	7	8	9	10	11*	12	14																1
1	2	3	4		6	14	8	9	10			5	7†	11														2
1	2	3	4	5	6*	12	8	9	10				11†	14	7													3
	2	3	4	5	6	12	8†	9	10				7*	11		1	14											4
1		3	4	5	6	12	8	9	10†	11			14	7*			2											5
1		3	4	5	6	7		9		11			10				8	2										6
1		3	4	5	6	7		9		11			10				8	2										7
1		3	4	5	6	10	2	9	12	7*			11				8											8
1		3	4	5	6	10	2†	9		11					7		8				14							9
1	5	3			6	2		9	10	11			4		7		8†				14							10
1	2*	3		5	6	12	7	9	10	11			4				8											11
1	2	3		5	6		4	9	10	11			14		7†		8											12
1		3	4		6	9	12	14	10	11†		2	5*		7		8											13
1		3		5	6	7		9*		11		2	4	10			8						12					14
1		3	4†	5	6*	11	2	9	10	12			7	14			8											15
1		3		5	6	4	7†	9	10	11			14				8					2						16
1		3		5	6	12		9	10	11*			4		7		8					2						17
1		3		5	6	10				11			4		7		8		9			2						18
1		3			6	4			10				12	11	7		8		9		2*	5						19
1		3		5	6	4	8	9	10				7	11								2						20
1		3	4	5	6		8	9	10	11					7							2						21
1		3	4	5	11	6		9†	10				14		7		8					2						22
1		3	4	5	6	11†	2	9	10				14		7		8											23
1		3	4*	5	6	2		9	10	12			11		7		8											24
1		3		5	6	12	8	9	10	14			4†	11	7*							2						25
1		3		5	6		8	9	10				4	11	7						2							26
1		3	4		6		8	9	10	11		5			7						2							27
1		3	4†		6			9	10	11		5	14	8*	7				12		2							28
1		3	4	5		7		9	10	11											2			6				29
1		3	4†	5	6	2		9	10	11			12		7*		8							14				30
1	2	3		5	6*	4		9	10	11			7	12			8†							14				31
	2	3		5	6	12	8	9	10					11*	7	1								4				32
		3*		5	6	8	2	9	10				12			1			11			7		4				33
1	2*	3		5	6	11†	9	12	10				14		7		8							4				34
		3*	4	5	6	2		9	10	11†			14		7	1	8							12				35
1		3	4	5	6	2		9	10	11†			14*		7		8							12				36
			4	5	6	14	2	9	10	11					7†	1	8							3				37
					6	12	2		10	11*					7	1	8		9					5	4	3		38
					6		2		10						7	1	8		9	11				5	4	3		39
1		3	4	5	6	2			10	11							8		9					7				40
			4		6	8			10	11		5	7†	14		1			9					2	3			41
1		3	4*	5	6	10				11		2	14				8		9	7†				12				42
			5		6*	12						3	7	11		1	8		14	10†				2		4	9	43
		3	4			8			10				7	11*		1			9	12				6	2	5		44
34	10	39	25	34	39	19	35	32	36	27		8	18	16	24	10	29	2	8	5	9	8		11	3	2	1	
						11	1	2	1	3		1	1	4	13		1		1			3		2			5	
		3	2	2	4	3	5	34	19	4			1	5	5		4							4	2			

1993-94

1	Aug	7	(h)	Hearts	W	2-1	Hagen, Hateley	42,320
2		14	(a)	St. Johnstone	W	2-1	Gough, Ferguson I	10,152
3		21	(a)	Celtic	D	0-0		47,942
4		28	(h)	Kilmarnock	L	1-2	Pressley	43,804
5	Sep	4	(a)	Dundee	D	1-1	Hateley	14,211
6		11	(h)	Partick T	D	1-1	Hateley	40,998
7		18	(a)	Aberdeen	L	0-2		19,138
8		25	(h)	Hibernian	W	2-1	Steven, Hateley	43,200
9	Oct	2	(a)	Raith R	D	1-1	Hetherston (og)	8,161
10		6	(h)	Motherwell	L	1-2	Ferguson I	39,816
11		9	(a)	Dundee U	W	3-1	Huistra 2, Hateley	11,262
12		16	(h)	St. Johnstone	W	2-0	Huistra, Hateley	41,960
13		30	(h)	Celtic	L	1-2	McCoist	47,522
14	Nov	3	(a)	Hearts	D	2-2	Hateley 2	18,370
15		6	(a)	Kilmarnock	W	2-0	Ferguson I, Huistra	19,157
16		10	(h)	Dundee	W	3-1	Ferguson I, McCoist 2 (1 pen)	38,477
17		13	(h)	Raith R	D	2-2	Hateley 2 (1 pen)	42,611
18		20	(a)	Hibernian	W	1-0	Gough	16,506
19		27	(a)	Partick T	D	1-1	Huistra	16,890
20	Dec	1	(h)	Aberdeen	W	2-0	Hateley 2	45,182
21		4	(a)	Motherwell	W	2-0	Durie 2	14,069
22		11	(h)	Dundee U	L	0-3		43,058
23		18	(a)	St. Johnstone	W	4-0	Hateley 2, Steven, Durie	10,056
24		27	(h)	Hearts	D	2-2	Hateley 2	45,116
25	Jan	1	(a)	Celtic	W	4-2	Hateley, Mikhailichenko 2, Kuznetsov	48,506
26		8	(h)	Kilmarnock	W	3-0	Huistra, Hateley 2	44,919
27		15	(a)	Dundee	D	1-1	Durie	10,864
28		22	(a)	Aberdeen	D	0-0		20,267
29	Feb	5	(h)	Partick T	W	5-1	Durie 2, Mikhailichenko, McCall, Steven	42,606
30		12	(h)	Hibernian	W	2-0	Durie, Steven	43,265
31		26	(a)	Raith R	W	2-1	Ferguson I, Durie	8,988
32	Mar	5	(h)	Motherwell	W	2-1	Durie, Hateley (pen)	43,669
33		19	(h)	St. Johnstone	W	4-0	McCall, Hateley, McPherson, Durie	43,228
34		26	(a)	Hearts	W	2-1	McCoist, Hateley	18,108
35		29	(a)	Partick T	W	2-1	Gough, McCoist	14,706
36	Apr	2	(h)	Aberdeen	D	1-1	McCall	45,888
37		5	(a)	Dundee U	D	0-0		11,352
38		16	(h)	Raith R	W	4-0	Robertson, McCoist, Ferguson D, Mikhailichenko	42,545
39		23	(h)	Dundee U	W	2-1	Durie 2	44,776
40		26	(a)	Motherwell	L	1-2	McCoist	14,050
41		30	(h)	Celtic	D	1-1	Mikhailichenko	47,018
42	May	3	(a)	Hibernian	L	0-1		14,517
43		7	(a)	Kilmarnock	L	0-1		18,012
44		14	(h)	Dundee	D	0-0		41,620

FINAL LEAGUE POSITION : 1st in Premier Division

Appearances

Sub. Appearances

Goals

60

Maxwell	McCall	Wishart	Gough	Pressley	Brown	Murray	Ferguson I	Hateley	Hagen	Mikhailichenko	Durrant	Huistra	Steven	Vinnicombe	McPherson	Ferguson D	Stevens	Robertson D	Kuznetsov	Morrow	Miller	McCoist	Scott	Durie	Goram	Moore	
1	2*	3	4	5	6	7	8	9	10	11†	12	14															1
1		3*	4	5	6	2	8†		9	12	10	11	7	14													2
1		3	4	2		6	8	10	14		12	11*	7		5	9†											3
1			4	5		6	8	10		11	12		7			9*	2	3									4
1			4	5			8	10			12	11*	7			9	2	3	6								5
1			4				8	10			12		7	6*	5	9	2	3		11							6
1	4				6		8	10				11*	7		5	12	2	3				9					7
1		6	4			14	8	10	9	11			7		5		2	3†									8
1*			4	5	3		8	10			6	11	7				2					9	12				9
			4	5	3		8	10	9*	14	6	12	7				2			11†			1				10
1	6		4	12			8*	10†			7	9	11		5		2	3				14					11
1			4				8	10		6	12	11	7		5		2	3				9*					12
1	6		4			14	8	10			12	11	7*		5		2†	3				9					13
1	2		4	14		6	8	10			7	11†			5			3				9					14
1	2		4†		14	6	8	10			7	11	12		5			3				9*					15
1			4			6	8	10		11	7	14			5		2	3				9†					16
1	5		4		6		8	10			7	9	11†				2	3			14						17
1	7		4		6	2	8	10			11	9			5			3									18
1	2		4		6		8*	10		11†	9	14			5	12		3						7			19
1	2		4†	14	6*	11	8	10			12		7		5			3				9					20
1	4*				6	11	8	10			12		7		5		2	3				9					21
1	6		4*	14		11	8	10			12		7		5†		2	3				9					22
1			4	5			8	10			11		7		3		2		6			9					23
1			4†	5	6	3		10		11	12		7	14			2		8			9*					24
1	8		4	5	6	3†		10		11	12		7				2		14			9*					25
1	8		4		6	5		10		11*	12		7				2	3				9					26
1	8			5	6	4		10		11*	12		7				2†	3	14			9					27
1	8		4		6	5		10		11	12		7				2	3				9*					28
1	8		4		6	5		10		11			7				2	3				9					29
	5		4		6		8	10		11			7				2	3				14		9†	1		30
			4		6		8	10		14			7		5		2	3				9†		11	1		31
	5		4		6		8	10		11†			7			12	2*	3				14		9	1		32
	2		4		6		8	10					7		5			3				9		11	1		33
	3		4		6		8	10		12			7		5		2					9		11*	1		34
	3		4		6		8	10		11†			7*		5	14	2					9		12	1		35
	7		4		6	3	8	10		12					5		2					9*		11	1		36
14	7		4		6	3				12			11	8*	5	10						9			1†	2	37
1	2		4		6		8	12		14			7		5	10		3*				9		11†			38
1	2		4		6		8	10					7		5			3				9		11			39
1	2		4		6		8			12			7		5*	10		3				9		11			40
	2		4			6*	8	10					7		5	14		3				9†	1	11			41
	2		4		6	14	8	10		11	9		7†		5*			3				12			1		42
		2	4	5				10			12	11	7†	14				3	6		8*	9	1				43
	6		4				8	10		12		11	7		5†		2	3				14	1	9*			44
31	34	5	37	17	24	20	35	40	4	24	14	10	32	2	27	7	28	32	4	2	2	16	5	23	8	1	
1			6		2		2	2	10	9	11		2	1	3	1		2		1	5	1	1				
	3		3	1		5		22	1	5	6	4			1	1		1	1			7		12			

1994-95

1	Aug	13	(h)	Motherwell	W	2-1	Hateley, Ferguson D	42,491
2		20	(a)	Partick T	W	2-0	Byrne (og), Hateley	14,361
3		27	(h)	Celtic	L	0-2		44,607
4	Sep	11	(h)	Hearts	W	3-0	Hateley 2 (1 pen), Durie	40,653
5		17	(a)	Falkirk	W	2-0	Boli, Laudrup	12,419
6		24	(a)	Aberdeen	D	2-2	Hateley, Moore	19,191
7	Oct	1	(h)	Dundee U	W	2-0	Hateley, Laudrup	43,635
8		8	(a)	Hibernian	L	1-2	Boli	12,088
9		15	(h)	Kilmarnock	W	2-0	Miller, Robertson D	44,099
10		22	(a)	Motherwell	L	1-2	Philiben (og)	11,160
11		30	(a)	Celtic	W	3-1	Hateley 2, Laudrup	32,171
12	Nov	5	(h)	Partick T	W	3-0	Laudrup, Miller, Hateley	43,696
13		9	(a)	Hearts	D	1-1	Hateley	12,347
14		19	(h)	Falkirk	D	1-1	Hateley	44,018
15		25	(h)	Aberdeen	W	1-0	McCoist	45,072
16	Dec	4	(a)	Dundee U	W	3-0	Laudrup, Huistra, Durrant	11,187
17		10	(a)	Kilmarnock	W	2-1	McLaren, Laudrup	17,219
18		26	(h)	Hibernian	W	2-0	Hateley, Gough	44,892
19		31	(a)	Motherwell	W	3-1	McCall, Laudrup, Durie	11,269
20	Jan	4	(h)	Celtic	D	1-1	Ferguson I	45,794
21		7	(a)	Partick T	D	1-1	Robertson D	17,298
22		14	(a)	Falkirk	W	3-2	Huistra 2 (1 pen), McCall	12,507
23		21	(h)	Hearts	W	1-0	Miller	44,231
24	Feb	4	(h)	Dundee U	D	1-1	Robertson D	44,197
25		12	(a)	Aberdeen	L	0-2		18,060
26		25	(h)	Kilmarnock	W	3-0	Durie, Laudrup, Durrant	44,859
27	Mar	4	(a)	Hibernian	D	1-1	Durie	11,939
28		11	(h)	Falkirk	D	2-2	Laudrup, Brown	43,359
29		18	(a)	Hearts	L	1-2	Laudrup	9,806
30	Apr	1	(a)	Dundee U	W	2-0	McLaren, Durie	11,035
31		8	(h)	Aberdeen	W	3-2	Durrant, Murray, Hateley	44,460
32		16	(h)	Hibernian	W	3-1	Durie, Durrant, Mikhailichenko	44,193
33		20	(a)	Kilmarnock	W	1-0	Mikhailichenko	16,532
34		29	(h)	Motherwell	L	0-2		43,576
35	May	7	(a)	Celtic	W	0-3		31,025
36		13	(h)	Partick T	D	1-1	Moore	45,280

FINAL LEAGUE POSITION : 1st in Premier Division

Appearances

Sub. Appearances

Goals

Murray	Robertson D	Gough	Boli	McPherson	Durrant	McCall	McCoist	Hateley	Laudrup	Ferguson D	Brown	Moore	Ferguson I	Pressley	Durie	Mikhailichenko	Miller	Huistra	Hagan	Wishart	McLaren	Scott	McGinty	Maxwell	Steven	Bollan	Cleland	Thomson	Robertson L	Caldwell	McKnight	
2	3	4	5	6	7	8	9†	10	11	14																						1
	4	5	6			2		10	11	9	3	7	8																			2
	4	5	6	7*		2		10	11	12		8	3		9																	3
7	3	4	5*	9	2			10	11†	14		6	8		12																	4
	3	4	5		7	2		10	11			6	8		9																	5
7	3	4	6	5		12	8*	10	11				2		9																	6
12	3	4	6	5	7	14		10	11			2				8*	9†															7
12	3	4*	6	5†	7	14		10	11			2					9	8														8
7	3	5	4					10	11			2			6		9	8														9
7†	3	6	5			4		10	11			2					9	8	14													10
8	3		6			4	14	10	11†								9*	7	12	2	5											11
8	3		6	12		4		10	11								9	7		2*	5											12
8†	3		6	9		4	14	10	11			2						7			5											13
	3		6	12		4	14	10	11			2					8*	7			5											14
	3		6	9		4	14	10†	11			2					8	7			5											15
	3	4	6	12		2		10	11						9*		8	7			5											16
6	3	4				2			11				14		9		8†	7			5											17
	3	4	6			2		10*	11		12				9		8	7			5	1										18
	3	4	6			2			11		10*	12			9		8	7			5	1										19
	3	4	6	14		2			11		12		8*		9		10†	7			5	1										20
11	3			9		4					6	2	8				7				5	15	10									21
10	3			11*		4					6	2†	8				9	7	14		5				1	12						22
10		4	6	12		2			11		3	14	8*		9						5				1	7†						23
	3	4	5		6	14		10	11		12	2			9†		8*								1	7						24
	3	4	5	12		8		10	11			2			14		9*								1		6†	7				25
	3*	4	6	14		2			11		12				10		9								1	7†		8				26
8*		4	6	12		10			11		2†	14			9						5				1	7	3					27
		4	6	7		2			11		10		8		9	14					5				1		3†					28
14		4	6	12		10			11				8		9						5				1	7*	3†	2				29
		4	6†	10	7				11		3				9*	12	8				5					14	2	1				30
12		4	6*	10		11†					3				9	14	8				5					7	2	1				31
12		4	6			10			11		3*				9†	14	8				5					7	2	1				32
6		4		9					11			2	8†		10						5				1		3	7	14			33
		4	6	9				10	11				8		3						5				1	7	2	1				34
14			4	9		10		11°			6†	2	8*		12						5	15	7			3	1					35
				9		10		11			4		8†		6						5	1°	7			3		2		14		36
14	23	25	28	9	15	30	4	23	33	1	10	19	13	2	17	4	21	15		3	24	3	1		10	10	5	10	5		1	App
6				10	5					3	3	2	3		4	5		2	1		1	1	1		1		1		1			Sub
1	3	1	2		4	2	1	13	10	1	1	2	1		6	2	3	3			2											Gls

63

SCOTTISH F.A. CUP

1970/71 SEASON
3rd Round
Jan 23 vs Falkirk (h) 3-0
Conn, Johnston 2
4th Round
Feb 13 vs St. Mirren (a) 3-1
Stein 2, Johnston (pen)
5th Round
Mar 6 vs Aberdeen (h) 1-0
Jackson
Semi-Final (at Hampden Park)
Mar 31 vs Hibernian 0-0
Replay
Apr 5 vs Hibernian 2-1
Henderson, Conn
FINAL (at Hampden Park)
May 9 vs Celtic 1-1
Att: 120,092 Johnstone D
Replay (at Hampden Park)
May 9 vs Celtic 1-2
Att: 103,332 Callaghan (og)

1971/72 SEASON
3rd Round
Feb 5 vs Falkirk (a) 2-2
Att: 20,000 Johnstone, Greig
Replay
Feb 9 vs Falkirk (h) 2-0
Att: 43,000 Stein, McLean
4th Round
Feb 26 vs St. Mirren (a) 4-1
Att: 29,376 MacDonald, Stein, McLean 2 (1 pen)
5th Round
Mar 18 vs Motherwell (a) 2-2
Att: 28,577 MacDonald, Stein
Replay
Mar 27 vs Motherwell (h) 4-2
Att: 40,000 Stein 2, McLean, Fallon (og)
Semi-Final (at Hampden Park)
Apr 15 vs Hibernian 1-1
Att: 75,884 MacDonald
Replay
Apr 24 vs Hibernian 0-2
Att: 58,000

1972/73 SEASON
3rd Round
Feb 3 vs Dundee United (h) 1-0
Att: 35,657 Young
4th Round
Feb 24 vs Hibernian (h) 1-1
Att: 63,889 Johnstone
Replay
Feb 28 vs Hibernian (a) 2-1
Att: 49,007 McLean 2 (1 pen)
5th Round
Mar 17 vs Airdrieonians (h) 2-0
Att: 35,000 Parlane (pen), Young
Semi-Final (at Hampden Park)
Apr 4 vs Ayr United 2-0
Att: 51,815 Parlane 2
FINAL (at Hampden Park)
May 5 vs Celtic 3-2
Att: 122,714 Parlane, Conn, Forsyth

1973/74 SEASON
3rd Round
Jan 26 vs Queen's Park (h) 8-0
Att: 19,000 Parlane 3, Scott, Morris, McLean 3
4th Round
Feb 17 vs Dundee (h) 0-3
Att: 65,000

1974/75 SEASON
3rd Round
Jan 25 vs Aberdeen (a) 1-1
Att: 30,000 Scott
Replay
Feb 10 vs Aberdeen (h) 1-2 (aet.)
Att: 50,000 McKean

1975/76 SEASON
3rd Round
Jan 24 vs East Fife (h) 3-0
Att: 30,000 MacDonald, Henderson, Hamilton
4th Round
Feb 14 vs Aberdeen (h) 4-1
Att: 53,000 Johnstone, MacDonald, Henderson, Parlane
5th Round
Mar 6 vs Queen of the South (a) 5-0
Att: 18,700 McKean 2, Johnstone 2, Hamilton
Semi-Final (at Hampden Park)
Mar 31 vs Motherwell 3-2
Att: 50,000 Miller (pen), Johnstone 2
FINAL (at Hampden Park)
May 1 vs Heart of Midlothian 3-1
Att: 85,354 Johnstone 2, MacDonald

1976/77 SEASON
3rd Round
Jan 29 vs Falkirk (h) 3-1
Att: 17,500 Jardine (pen), Johnstone, MacDonald
4th Round
Feb 26 vs Elgin City (h) 3-0
Att: 18,000 Jackson, McLean (pen), MacDonald
5th Round
Mar 12 vs Motherwell (h) 2-0
Att: 35,572 McKean, Watson
Semi-Final (at Hampden Park)
Mar 30 vs Heart of Midlothian 2-0
Att: 23,222 Jackson, Jardine (pen)
FINAL (at Hampden Park)
May 7 vs Celtic 0-1
Att: 54,252

1977/78 SEASON
3rd Round
Jan 28 vs Berwick Rangers (a) 4-2
Att: 10,500 Johnstone 2, Jackson 2
4th Round
Feb 18 vs Stirling Albion (h) 1-0
Att: 15,000 Johnstone
5th Round
Mar 11 vs Kilmarnock (h) 4-1
Att: 28,000 Johnstone, Hamilton, MacDonald, Cooper (pen)
Semi-Final (at Hampden Park)
Apr 5 vs Dundee United 2-0
Att: 25,619 Johnstone, Greig
FINAL (at Hampden Park)
May 6 vs Aberdeen 2-1
Att: 61,563 MacDonald, Johnstone

1978/79 SEASON
3rd Round
Feb 12 vs Motherwell (h) 3-1
Att: 12,000 Johnstone, Cooper, Jackson
4th Round
Feb 21 vs Kilmarnock (h) 1-1
Att: 17,500 McDonald
Replay
Feb 26 vs Kilmarnock (a) 1-0
Att: 16,000 Urquhart
5th Round
Mar 10 vs Dundee (h) 6-3
Att: 25,000 Jardine (pen), Forsyth T, Smith,

MacDonald, Russell, Cooper
Semi-Final (at Hampden Park)
Apr 4 vs Partick Thistle 0-0
Att: 26,232
Replay (at Hampden Park)
Apr 16 vs Partick Thistle 1-0
Att: 32,300 Johnstone
FINAL (at Hampden Park)
May 12 vs Hibernian 0-0
Att: 50,610
Replay (at Hampden Park)
May 16 vs Hibernian 0-0 (aet.)
Att: 33,504
2nd Replay (at Hampden Park)
May 28 vs Hibernian 3-2 (aet.)
Att: 30,602 Johnstone 2, Duncan (og)

1979/80 SEASON
3rd Round
Jan 26 vs Clyde (a) 2-2
Att: 12,500 Jackson, Jardine (pen)
Replay
Jan 30 vs Clyde (h) 2-0
Att: 10,000 MacDonald J 2
4th Round
Feb 16 vs Dundee United (h) 1-0
Att: 25,000 Johnstone
5th Round
Mar 8 vs Heart of Midlothian (h) 6-1
Att: 31,000 MacDonald J 2, Jardine (pen), Cooper, Johnstone, Russell
Semi-Final (at Celtic Park)
Apr 12 vs Aberdeen 1-0
Att: 44,000 Johnstone
FINAL (at Hampden Park)
May 10 vs Celtic 0-1
Att: 70,303

1980/81 SEASON
3rd Round
Jan 24 vs Airdrieonians (a) 5-0
Att: 16,054 Stevens, Redford, Bett, Johnstone 2
4th Round
Feb 14 vs St. Johnstone (a) 3-3
Att: 17,595 McAdam, Redford 2
Replay
Feb 18 vs St. Johnstone (h) 3-1
Att: 23,000 McAdam 2, Stevens
5th Round
Mar 7 vs Hibernian (h) 3-1
Att: 25,690 Russell, McAdam, MacDonald
Semi-Final (at Celtic Park)
Apr 11 vs Morton 2-1
Att: 27,050 Jackson, Russell
FINAL (at Hampden Park)
May 9 vs Dundee United 0-0 (aet.)
Att: 53,000
Replay (at Hampden Park)
May 12 vs Dundee United 4-1
Att: 43,099 Cooper, Russell, MacDonald 2

1981/82 SEASON
3rd Round
Feb 6 vs Albion Rovers (h) 6-2
Att: 10,000 Johnstone, Russell, MacDonald, McAdam, McPherson (pen), Redford
4th Round
Feb 13 vs Dumbarton (h) 4-0
Att: 12,000 Jardine 2, McAdam, Johnstone
5th Round
Mar 6 vs Dundee (h) 2-0
Att: 16,500 Johnstone, McAdam
Semi-Final (at Hampden Park)
Apr 3 vs Forfar Athletic 0-0
Att: 15,878

Replay (at Hampden Park)
Apr 6 vs Forfar Athletic 3-1
Att: 11,864 Johnstone, Bett, Cooper

FINAL (at Hampden Park)
May 22 vs Aberdeen 1-4 (aet.)
Att: 53,788 MacDonald

1982/83 SEASON
3rd Round
Jan 28 vs Falkirk (a) 2-0
Att: 15,000 Oliver (og), Kennedy

4th Round
Feb 19 vs Forfar Athletic (h) 2-1
Att: 12,500 MacDonald 2

5th Round
Mar 12 vs Queen's Park (a) 2-1
Att: 13,716 Dalziel, Cooper

Semi-Final (at Celtic Park)
Apr 16 vs St. Mirren 1-1
Att: 31,102 Clark

Replay (at Hampden Park)
Apr 19 vs St. Mirren 1-0 (aet.)
Att: 25,125 Clark

FINAL (at Hampden Park)
May 21 vs Aberdeen 0-1 (aet.)
Att: 62,979

1983/84 SEASON
3rd Round
Jan 28 vs Dunfermline Athletic (h) 2-1
Att: 18,000 McAdam, McCoist

4th Round
Feb 18 vs Inverness Caledonian (a) 6-0
Att: 5,500 Redford, Williamson 2, Russell, McCoist 2

5th Round
Mar 10 vs Dundee (a) 2-2
Att: 17,097 McGeachie (og), Russell

Replay
Mar 17 vs Dundee (h) 2-3
Att: 25,000 McClelland, McPherson

1984/85 SEASON
3rd Round
Jan 26 vs Morton (a) 3-3
Att: 12,012 Prytz, MacDonald, McPherson

Replay
Jan 30 vs Morton (h) 3-1
Att: 18,166 Mitchell, Fraser C, MacDonald

4th Round
Feb 16 vs Dundee (h) 0-1
Att: 26,619

1985/86 SEASON
3rd Round
Jan 25 vs Heart of Midlothian (a) 2-3
Att: 27,500 McCoist, Durrant

1986/87 SEASON
3rd Round
Jan 31 vs Hamilton Acad. (h) 0-1
Att: 35,462

1987/88 SEASON
3rd Round
Feb 8 vs Raith Rovers (a) 0-0
Att: 9,500

Replay
Feb 10 vs Raith Rovers (h) 4-1
Att: 35,144 Durrant 2 (1 pen), McCoist, Walters

4th Round
Feb 20 vs Dunfermline Athletic (a) 0-2
Att: 19,000

1988/89 SEASON
3rd Round
Jan 28 vs Raith Rovers (a) 1-1
Att: 10,000 Ferguson I

Replay
Feb 1 vs Raith Rovers (h) 3-0
Att: 40,307 Walters, Drinkell, Fraser (og)

4th Round
Feb 18 vs Stranraer (h) 8-0
Att: 41,198 Ferguson I, Drinkell 2, Brown 2, McCoist 2 (1 pen), Walters

5th Round
Mar 21 vs Dundee United (h) 2-2
Att: 42,177 Drinkell, McCoist

Replay
Mar 27 vs Dundee United (a) 1-0
Att: 21,872 McCoist

Semi-Final (at Celtic Park)
Apr 15 vs St. Johnstone 0-0
Att: 47,374

Replay (at Celtic Park)
Apr 19 vs St. Johnstone 4-0
Att: 44,205 Walters, Stevens, Drinkell, McCoist

FINAL (at Hampden Park)
May 20 vs Celtic 0-1
Att: 72,069

1989/90 SEASON
3rd Round
Jan 20 vs St. Johnstone (h) 3-0
Att: 39,003 Johnston, Brown, Walters

4th Round
Feb 25 vs Celtic (a) 0-1
Att: 53,000

1990/91 SEASON
3rd Round
Jan 29 vs Dunfermline Athletic (h) 2-0
Att: 29,003 Huistra, Spackman

4th Round
Feb 23 vs Cowdenbeath (h) 5-0
Att: 29,527 Hateley 2, Nisbet, McCoist, Walters (pen)

5th Round
Mar 17 vs Celtic (h) 0-2
Att: 52,000

1991/92 SEASON
3rd Round
Jan 22 vs Aberdeen (a) 1-0
Att: 23,000 McCoist

4th Round
Feb 15 vs Motherwell (h) 2-1
Att: 38,444 Mikhailichenko 2

5th Round
Mar 3 vs St. Johnstone (a) 3-0
Att: 10,107 McCoist, Gough, Hateley

Semi-Final (at Hampden Park)
Mar 31 vs Celtic 1-0
Att: 45,191 McCoist

FINAL (at Hampden Park)
May 9 vs Airdrieonians 2-1
Att: 44,045 Hateley, McCoist

1992/93 SEASON
3rd Round
Jan 9 vs Motherwell (a) 2-0
Att: 14,314 McCoist 2

4th Round
Feb 6 vs Ayr United (a) 2-0
Att: 13,176 McCoist, Gordon

5th Round
Mar 6 vs Arbroath (a) 3-0
Att: 6,488 Hateley, Murray, McCoist (pen)

Semi-Final (at Celtic Park)
Apr 3 vs Heart of Midlothian 2-1
Att: 41,738 McPherson, McCoist

FINAL (at Celtic Park)
May 29 vs Aberdeen 2-1
Att: 50,715 Murray, Hateley

1993/94 SEASON
3rd Round
Jan 29 vs Dumbarton (h) 4-1
Att: 36,671 Durie, Hateley (pen), Steven, Robertson

4th Round
Feb 19 vs Alloa Athletic (h) 6-0
Att: 37,620 Ferguson I, McPherson, McCoist 3 (1 pen), Mewbigging (og)

5th Round
Mar 12 vs Heart of Midlothian (h) 2-0
Att: 41,666 Brown, Hateley

Semi-Final (at Hampden Park)
Apr 10 vs Kilmarnock 0-0
Att: 35,134

Replay (at Hampden Park)
Apr 13 vs Kilmarnock 2-1
Att: 29,860 Hateley 2

FINAL (at Hampden Park)
May 21 vs Dundee 0-1
Att: 37,450

1994/95 SEASON
3rd Round
Feb 6 vs Hamilton Acad. (a) 3-1
Att: 18,379 Steven, Boli, Laudrup

4th Round
Feb 20 vs Heart of Midlothian (a) 2-4
Att: 12,375 Laudrup, Durie

SCOTTISH LEAGUE CUP

1970/71 SEASON
Preliminary Round, Game One
Aug 8 vs Dunfermline Athletic (h) 4-1
Att: 45,000 Stein 2, Jardine, Johnston

Preliminary Round, Game Two
Aug 12 vs Motherwell (a) 2-0
Att: -   Fyfe, Henderson

Preliminary Round, Game Three
Aug 15 vs Morton (h) 0-0
Att: 35,000

Preliminary Round, Game Four
Aug 19 vs Motherwell (h) 2-0
Att: -   Penman, Stein

Preliminary Round, Game Five
Aug 22 vs Dunfermline Athletic (a) 6-0
Att: 17,000 Johnston 3, Stein, Jackson, Fyfe

Preliminary Round, Game Six
Aug 26 vs Morton (a) 2-0
Att: 18,000 Johnston, Conn

Quarter-Final (1st leg)
Sep 9 vs Hibernian (h) 3-1
Att: 37,355 Conn, Fyfe 2

Quarter-Final (2nd leg)
Aug 23 vs Hibernian (h) 3-1 (agg. 6-2)
Att: -   McDonald, Greig, Fyfe

Semi-Final (at Hampden Park)
Oct 14 vs Cowdenbeath 2-0
Att: 32,000 Johnston, Smith

FINAL (at Hampden Park)
Oct 24 vs Celtic 1-0
Att: 106,263 Johnstone

1971/72 SEASON
Preliminary Round, Game One
Aug 14 vs Celtic (a) 0-2
Att: 73,000

Preliminary Round, Game Two
Aug 18 vs Ayr United (h) 4-0
Att: 25,000 Johnstone 2, Stein, McLean

Preliminary Round, Game Three
Aug 21 vs Morton (h) 2-0
Att: 32,000 Johnstone, Macdonald

Preliminary Round, Game Four
Aug 25 vs Ayr United (a) 4-0
Att: 15,000 Macdonald, Stein 2, Johnstone

Preliminary Round, Game Five
Aug 28 vs Celtic (h) 0-3
Att: 74,000

Preliminary Round, Game Six
Sep 1 vs Morton (a) 1-0
Att: 7,000 Stein

1972/73 SEASON
Preliminary Round, Game One
Aug 12 vs Clydebank (h) 2-0
Att: 25,000 Conn, Macdonald

Preliminary Round, Game Two
Aug 16 vs St. Mirren (a) 4-0
Att: 12,000 Johnston W, Greig, Stein, Conn

Preliminary Round, Game Three
Aug 19 vs Ayr United (h) 2-1
Att: 20,000 Johnston, Parlane

Preliminary Round, Game Four
Aug 23 vs St. Mirren (h) 1-4
Att: 15,000 Conn

Preliminary Round, Game Five
Aug 26 vs Clydebank (a) 5-0
Att: 8,000 Greig, McLean, Smith, Johnstone, Stein

Preliminary Round, Game Six
Aug 30 vs Ayr United (a) 2-1
Att: 14,000 Johnston, Johnstone

2nd Round (1st leg)
Sep 20 vs Stenhousemuir (a) 5-0
Att: 3,650 Johnstone D 3, Parlane, Greig

2nd Round (2nd leg)
Oct 4 vs Stenhousemuir (h) 1-2 (agg. 6-2)
Att: 3,000 Fyfe

Quarter-Final (1st leg)
Oct 11 vs St. Johnstone (h) 1-1
Att: 15,000 Parlane

Quarter-Final (2nd leg)
Nov 1 vs St. Johnstone (a) 2-0 (agg. 3-1)
Att: 13,000 Young, Parlane

Semi-Final (at Hampden Park)
Nov 22 vs Hibernian 0-1
Att: 46,513

1973/74 SEASON
Preliminary Round, Game One
Aug 11 vs Falkirk (h) 3-1
Att: 30,000 Scott 2, Conn

Preliminary Round, Game Two
Aug 15 vs Arbroath (a) 2-1
Att: 6,677 Conn, Parlane

Preliminary Round, Game Three
Aug 18 vs Celtic (h) 1-2
Att: 60,000 Scott

Preliminary Round, Game Four
Aug 22 vs Arbroath (h) 3-0
Att: 10,000 Macdonald, Conn, Smith

Preliminary Round, Game Five
Aug 25 vs Celtic (a) 3-1
Att: 57,000 Macdonald, Parlane, Conn

Preliminary Round, Game Six
Aug 29 vs Falkirk (a) 5-1
Att: 12,000 O'Hara, McLean, Forsyth, Conn 2

2nd Round (1st leg)
Sep 12 vs Dumbarton (h) 6-0
Att: 10,000 Parlane 3, Young 2, Greig

2nd Round (2nd leg)
Oct 10 vs Dumbarton (a) 2-1 (agg. 8-1)
Att: 6,000 Scott, Fyfe

Quarter-Final (1st leg)
Oct 31 vs Hibernian (h) 2-0
Att: 22,000 Greig, Schaedler (og)

Quarter-Final (2nd leg)
Nov 21 vs Hibernian (a) 0-0 (agg. 2-0)
Att: 19,245

Semi-Final (at Hampden Park)
Dec 5 vs Celtic 1-3
Att: 54,864 MacDonald

1974/75 SEASON
Preliminary Round, Game One
Aug 7 vs St. Johnstone (h) 3-2
Att: 20,000 Scott, Jardine, Parlane

Preliminary Round, Game Two
Aug 10 vs Hibernian (a) 1-3
Att: 23,539 Scott

Preliminary Round, Game Three
Aug 14 vs St. Johnstone (a) 6-3
Att: 6,000 Young 2, Jardine 2, Scott, Forsyth

Preliminary Round, Game Four
Aug 17 vs Dundee (a) 2-0
Att: 18,548 Jardine, Fyfe

Preliminary Round, Game Five
Aug 24 vs Dundee (h) 4-0
Att: 35,000 Jardine, Scott, Johnstone 2

Preliminary Round, Game Six
Aug 28 vs Hibernian (h) 0-1
Att: 55,000

1975/76 SEASON
Preliminary Round, Game One
Aug 9 vs Airdrieonians (h) 6-1
Att: 45,000 Jardine 3, Miller, Stein, Parlane

Preliminary Round, Game Two
Aug 13 vs Clyde (h) 1-0
Att: 28,000 Johnstone

Preliminary Round, Game Three
Aug 16 vs Motherwell (h) 1-1
Att: 30,000 Greig

Preliminary Round, Game Four
Aug 20 vs Clyde (h) 1-0
Att: 15,000 Miller, Jackson, MacDonald, Parlane 2, Young

Preliminary Round, Game Five
Aug 23 vs Motherwell (a) 2-2
Att: 20,561 Jardine, Miller

Preliminary Round, Game Six
Aug 27 vs Airdrieonians (a) 2-1
Att: 20,000 Johnstone, Young

Quarter-Final (1st leg)
Sep 10 vs Queen of the South (h) 1-0
Att: 12,000 Johnstone

Quarter-Final (2nd leg)
Sep 24 vs Queen of the South (a) 2-2 (aet.)
(90 minutes 1-2) (aggregate 3-2)
Att: 7,500 Johnstone, MacDonald

Semi-Final (at Hampden Park)
Oct 8 vs Montrose 5-1
Att: 20,319 Jardine, Miller, Scott, Johnstone, Parlane

FINAL (at Hampden Park)
Oct 25 vs Celtic 1-0
Att: 58,806 MacDonald

1976/77 SEASON
Preliminary Round, Game One
Aug 14 vs St. Johnstone (h) 5-0
Att: 25,000 Jardine 2, Johnstone, Miller, Henderson

Preliminary Round, Game Two
Aug 18 vs Hibernian (a) 1-1
Att: 25,000 Munro

Preliminary Round, Game Three
Aug 21 vs Montrose (h) 4-0
Att: 18,500 Johnstone 2, Jardine, Mac-Donald

Preliminary Round, Game Four
Aug 25 vs Hibernian (h) 3-0
Att: 45,000 Miller, Jardine, McLean

Preliminary Round, Game Five
Aug 28 vs Montrose (a) 3-0
Att: 7,000 Johnstone, Parlane, Jardine

Preliminary Round, Game Six
Sep 1 vs St. Johnstone (a) 1-0
Att: 4,070 Jardine

Quarter-Final (1st leg)
Sep 22 vs Clydebank (h) 3-3
Att: 12,000 Johnstone, MacDonald, Hamilton

Quarter-Final (2nd leg)
Oct 6 vs Clydebank (a) 1-1 (aet.) (agg. 4-4)
Att: 10,000 Greig

Replay (at Dens Park)
Oct 18 vs Clydebank 0-0 (aet.)
Att: 15,000

2nd Replay (at Firhill Park)
Oct 19 vs Clydebank 3-1
Att: 14,000 Parlane, McKean

Semi-Final (at Hampden Park)
Oct 27 vs Aberdeen 1-5
Att: 20,990 MacDonald

1977/78 SEASON
2nd Round (1st leg)
Aug 24 vs St. Johnstone (h) 3-1
Att: 5,000 Johnstone 2, Miller

2nd Round (2nd leg)
Sep 3 vs St. Johnstone (a) 3-0 (agg. 6-1)
Att: 11,000 Miller, Smith, Parlane

3rd Round (1st leg)
Oct 5 vs Aberdeen (h) 6-1
Att: 20,000 MacDonald, Johnstone, Smith 3, Miller

3rd Round (2nd leg)
Oct 26 vs Aberdeen (a) 1-3 (aggregate 7-4)
Att: 15,600 Smith

Quarter-Final (1st leg)
Nov 9 vs Dunfermline Athletic (h) 3-1
Att: 10,000 McLean 2, Jackson

Quarter-Final (2nd leg)
Nov 16 vs Dunfermline A. (a) 3-1 (agg. 6-2)
Att: 10,000 Jardine, Johnstone, Greig

Semi-Final (at Hampden Park)
Feb 27 vs Forfar Athletic 5-2 (aet.)
Att: 30,000 Johnstone 2, Parlane 2, Mac-Donald

FINAL (at Hampden Park)
Mar 18 vs Celtic 2-1 (aet.)
Att: 60,168 Cooper, Smith

1978/79 SEASON
1st Round (1st leg)
Aug 16 vs Albion Rovers (h) 3-0
Att: 10,000 Parlane, Smith, Johnstone

1st Round (2nd leg)
Aug 23 vs Albion Rovers (a) 1-0 (agg. 4-0)
Att: 6,500 Parlane

2nd Round (1st leg)
Aug 30 vs Forfar Athletic (h) 3-0
Att: 5,000 Smith, Cooper, McLean

2nd Round (2nd leg)
Sep 2 vs Forfar Athletic (a) 4-1 (agg. 7-1)
Att: 5,919 Cooper, Smith 2, MacDonald

3rd Round (1st leg)
Oct 4 vs St. Mirren (h) 3-2
Att: 18,000 Cooper, Miller, Johnstone

3rd Round (2nd leg)
Oct 11 vs St. Mirren (a) 0-0 (agg. 3-2)
Att: 16,000

Quarter-Final (1st leg)
Nov 8 vs Arbroath (h) 1-0
Att: 10,000 Wells (og)

Quarter-Final (2nd leg)
Nov 15 vs Arbroath (a) 2-1 (aggregate 3-1)
Att: 4,000 Smith, Russell

mi-Final (at Hampden Park)
ec 13 vs Celtic 3-2 (aet.)
e: 49,432 Jardine, Jackson, Casey (og)

NAL (at Hampden Park)
ar 31 vs Aberdeen 2-1
e: 54,000 McMaster (og), Jackson

)79/80 SEASON

d Round (1st leg)
ig 29 vs Clyde (a) 2-1
e: 5,021 Dawson, Robertson

d Round (2nd leg)
ip 1 vs Clyde (h) 4-0 (aggregate 6-1)
i: 14,000 Smith, Mackay 2, O'Neill (og)

d Round (1st leg)
p 26 vs Aberdeen (a) 1-3
i: 18,000 Johnstone

d Round (2nd leg)
ct 10 vs Aberdeen (h) 0-2 (aggregate 1-5)
i: 28,000

)80/81 SEASON

d Round (1st leg)
ig 27 vs Forfar Athletic (a) 2-0
i: 4,500 McAdam 2

d Round (2nd leg)
ig 30 vs Forfar Athletic (h) 3-1 (agg. 5-1)
i: 15,000 Miller, Johnstone, McAdam

d Round (1st leg)
p 3 vs Aberdeen (h) 1-0
i: 30,000 McAdam

d Round (2nd leg)
p 24 vs Aberdeen (a) 1-3 (aggregate 2-3)
i: 19,000 McAdam

)81/82 SEASON

eliminary Round, Game One
ig 8 vs Morton (a) 1-1
t: 14,000 McAdam

eliminary Round, Game Two
ig 12 vs Dundee (h) 4-1
t: 13,500 MacDonald, Miller, Johnstone, cAdam

eliminary Round, Game Three
ig 15 vs Raith Rovers (h) 8-1
t: 16,000 Jardine, Russell 2, McAdam, dford 4

eliminary Round, Game Four
ig 19 vs Dundee (a) 2-1
t: 9,124 McGeachie (og), Stevens

eliminary Round, Game Five
ig 22 vs Morton (h) 1-0
t: 23,000 Johnstone

eliminary Round, Game Six
ig 26 vs Raith Rovers (a) 3-1
t: 6,000 Redford, Johnstone, MacDonald

uarter-Final (1st leg)
ip 2 vs Brechin City (a) 4-0
i:7,000 Russell, Jackson, McLean, Redford

uarter-Final (2nd leg)
ip 23 vs Brechin City (h) 1-0 (agg. 5-0)
t: 2,000 MacDonald

mi-Final (1st leg)
ct 7 vs St. Mirren (a) 2-2
t: 14,058 McAdam, MacDonald

mi-Final (2nd leg)
ct 28 vs St. Mirren (h) 2-1 (aggregate 4-3)
t: 17,000 Bett, MacDonald

NAL (at Hampden Park)
ov 28 vs Dundee United 2-1
t: 53,777 Cooper, Redford

)82/83 SEASON

reliminary Round, Game One
ug 14 vs Hibernian (a) 1-1
t: 15,980 MacDonald

Preliminary Round, Game Two
Aug 18 vs Airdrieonians (h) 3-1
Att: 9,500 Bett, Paterson, Black

Preliminary Round, Game Three
Aug 21 vs Clydebank (a) 4-1
Att: 7,090 Prytz, MacDonald 2, McClelland

Preliminary Round, Game Four
Aug 25 vs Airdrieonians (a) 2-1
Att: 6,476 Dalziel, Paterson

Preliminary Round, Game Five
Aug 28 vs Hibernian (h) 0-0
Att: 17,600

Preliminary Round, Game Six
Sep 1 vs Clydebank (h) 3-2
Att: 6,300 MacDonald, Redford, Prytz (pen)

Quarter-Final (1st leg)
Sep 22 vs Kilmarnock (a) 6-1
Att: 5,500 Cooper 4, MacDonald 2

Quarter-Final (2nd leg)
Oct 6 vs Kilmarnock (h) 6-0 (agg. 12-1)
Att: 5,000 MacDonald 2, Johnstone 2, McPherson, Bett

Semi-Final (1st leg)
Oct 27 vs Heart of Midlothian (h) 2-0
Att: 25,000 Cooper, Bett

Semi-Final (2nd leg)
Nov 10 vs Heart of Midl. (a) 2-1 (agg. 4-1)
Att: 18,983 Bett, Johnstone

FINAL (at Hampden Park)
Dec 4 vs Celtic 1-2
Att: 55,372 Bett

1983/84 SEASON

2nd Round (1st leg)
Aug 24 vs Queen of the South (h) 4-0
Att: 8,000 Prytz, Clark, MacDonald 2

2nd Round (2nd leg)
Aug 27 vs Queen of South (a) 4-1 (agg. 8-1)
Att: 7,350 Mitchell, MacKinnon, Cooper, McCoist

3rd Round, Game One
Aug 31 vs Clydebank (h) 4-0
Att: 7,000 McCoist 2, Russell, Prytz

3rd Round, Game Two
Sep 7 vs Heart of Midlothian (a) 3-0
Att: 11,287 Clark 2, Gauld (og)

3rd Round, Game Three
Oct 5 vs St. Mirren (h) 5-0
Att: 10,000 McCoist 2, Clark, McClelland, Paterson

3rd Round, Game Four
Oct 26 vs Heart of Midlothian (h) 2-0
Att: 5,000 Prytz, Mitchell

3rd Round, Game Five
Nov 9 vs Clydebank (h) 3-0
Att: 3,612 Cooper, McCoist, McPherson

3rd Round, Game Six
Nov 30 vs St. Mirren (a) 1-0
Att: 4,536 Cooper

Semi-Final (1st leg)
Feb 14 vs Dundee United (a) 1-1
Att: 14,569 Mitchell

Semi-Final (2nd leg)
Feb 22 vs Dundee United (h) 2-0 (agg. 3-1)
Att: 35,950 Clark, Redford

FINAL (at Hampden Park)
Mar 25 vs Celtic 3-2 (aet.)
Att: 66,369 McCoist 3

1984/85 SEASON

2nd Round
Aug 22 vs Falkirk (h) 1-0
Att: 8,000 McPherson

3rd Round
Aug 29 vs Raith Rovers (h) 4-0
Att: 6,000 McCoist 2, Paterson, Redford

Quarter-Final
Sep 5 vs Cowdenbeath (a) 3-1
Att: 9,925 Ferguson I, Russell, Redford

Semi-Final (1st leg)
Sep 26 vs Meadowbank (h) 4-0
Att: 15,000 McCoist 2, Ferguson, Fraser

Semi-Final (2nd leg)
Oct 9 vs Meadowbank (a) 1-1 (agg. 5-1)
Att: 5,100 McCoist

FINAL (at Hampden Park)
Oct 28 vs Dundee United 1-0
Att: 44,698 Ferguson

1985/86 SEASON

2nd Round
Aug 21 vs Clyde (h) 5-0
Att: 11,350 McCoist, Williamson 3 (1 pen), Paterson

3rd Round
Aug 27 vs Forfar Athletic (a) 2-2 (aet.)
Att: 7,282 Cooper (pen), Williamson
Rangers won 6-5 on penalties

Quarter-Final
Sep 4 vs Hamilton Academical (a) 2-1
Att: 12,392 Williamson 2

Semi-Final (1st leg)
Sep 25 vs Hibernian (a) 0-2
Att: 18,000

Semi-Final (2nd leg)
Oct 9 vs Hibernian (h) 1-0 (aggregate 1-2)
Att: 38,000 Cooper

1986/87 SEASON

2nd Round
Aug 20 vs Stenhousemuir (a) 4-1
Att: 9,052 Souness, West, Cooper, McCoist

3rd Round
Aug 27 vs East Fife (h) 0-0 (aet.)
Att: 8,835 Rangers won 5-4 on penalties

Quarter-Final
Sep 3 vs Dundee (h) 3-1 (aet.)
Att: 33,712 Fraser, Souness, McMinn

Semi-Final (at Hampden Park)
Sep 24 vs Dundee United 2-1
Att: 45,249 McCoist, McMinn

FINAL (at Hampden Park)
Oct 26 vs Celtic 2-1
Att: 74,219 Durrant, Cooper (pen)

1987/88 SEASON

2nd Round
Aug 19 vs Stirling Albion (a) 2-1
Att: 13,000 Falco, McCoist

3rd Round
Aug 26 vs Dunfermline Athletic (a) 4-1
Att: 18,070 McCoist 3 (1 pen), Falco

Quarter-Final
Sep 2 vs Heart of Midlothian (h) 4-1
Att: 39,303 Durrant 2, McCoist 2 (1 pen)

Semi-Final (at Hampden Park)
Sep 23 vs Motherwell 3-1
Att: 45,938 Kirk (og), Fleck, Falco

FINAL (at Hampden Park)
Oct 25 vs Aberdeen 3-3 (aet.)
Att: 71,961 Bett (pen), Hewitt, Falco
Rangers won 5-3 on penalties

1988/89 SEASON

2nd Round
Aug 17 vs Clyde (a) 3-0
Att: 14,699 Drinkell, Walters, Ferguson D

3rd Round
Aug 23 vs Clydebank (h) 6-0
Att: 34,376 McCoist, Gough, Walters, Wilkins, Drinkell, Durrant

Semi-Final (at Hampden Park)
Sep 21 vs Heart of Midlothian 3-0
Att: 53,623 Walters 2, Nisbet

FINAL (at Hampden Park)
Oct 23 vs Aberdeen 3-2
Att: 72,122 McCoist 2 (1 pen), Ferguson I

1989/90 SEASON
2nd Round
Aug 15 vs Arbroath (h) 4-0
Att: 31,762 McCoist 3, Ferguson
3rd Round
Aug 23 vs Morton (a) 2-1
Att: 11,821 Walters, Pickering (og)
Quarter-Final
Aug 30 vs Hamilton Academical (a) 3-0
Att: 9,162 Walters 2 (1 pen), Steven
Semi-Final (at Hampden Park)
Sep 19 vs Dunfermline Athletic 5-0
Att: 41,643 Steven, Johnston, McCoist 2, Ferguson I
FINAL (at Hampden Park)
Oct 22 vs Aberdeen 1-2 (aet.)
Att: 61,190 Walters (pen)

1990/91 SEASON
2nd Round
Aug 21 vs East Stirling (h) 5-0
Att: 25,595 Steven, Hateley 2, Walters, Johnston
3rd Round
Aug 28 vs Kilmarnock (h) 1-0
Att: 32,671 Johnston
Quarter-Final
Sep 4 vs Raith Rovers (h) 6-2
Att: 31,230 McCoist 3, Johnston, Butcher, Steven
Semi-Final (at Hampden Park)
Sep 26 vs Aberdeen 1-0
Att: 40,855 Steven
FINAL (at Hampden Park)
Oct 28 vs Celtic 2-1 (aet.)
Att: 62,817 Walters, Gough

1991/92 SEASON
2nd Round
Aug 20 vs Queen's Park (h) 6-0
Att: 32,230 Durrant, Johnston 4, Spackman
3rd Round
Aug 28 vs Partick Thistle (a) 2-0
Att: 12,587 Johnston, Robertson D
Quarter-Final
Sep 4 vs Heart of Midlothian (a) 1-0
Att: 22,878 McCoist
Semi-Final (at Hampden Park)
Sep 25 vs Hibernian 0-1
Att: 40,901

1992/93 SEASON
2nd Round (at Hampden Park)
Aug 11 vs Dumbarton (a) 5-0
Att: 11,090 Durrant, Gordon, Hateley, McCoist, Mikhailichenko
3rd Round
Aug 19 vs Stranraer (a) 5-0
Att: 4,430 Hateley 2, McCoist 3
Quarter-Final
Aug 26 vs Dundee United (a) 3-2 (aet.)
Att: 15,716 McCoist, Gough, Huistra
Semi-Final (at Hampden Park)
Sep 22 vs St. Johnstone 3-1
Att: 30,062 McCoist 3
FINAL (at Hampden Park)
Oct 25 vs Aberdeen 2-1
Att: 45,298 McCall, Smith (og)

1993/94 SEASON
2nd Round
Aug 11 vs Dumbarton (h) 1-0
Att: 36,309 Ferguson I

3rd Round
Aug 24 vs Dunfermline Athletic (a) 2-0
Att: 12,993 Steven, Ferguson I
Quarter-Final
Sep 1 vs Aberdeen (h) 2-1 (aet.)
Att: 44,928 Hateley (pen), Ferguson I
Semi-Final (at Ibrox Stadium)
Sep 22 vs Celtic 1-0
Att: 47,420 Hateley
FINAL (at Celtic Park)
Oct 24 vs Hibernian 2-1
Att: 47,632 Durrant, McCoist

1994/95 SEASON
2nd Round
Aug 17 vs Arbroath (a) 6-1
Att: 4,556 Hateley 2, Ferguson D 3, McCall
3rd Round
Aug 31 vs Falkirk (h) 1-2
Att: 40,741 Laudrup

EUROPEAN CUP

1975/76 SEASON
1st Round (1st leg)
Sep 17 vs Bohemians Dublin (h) 4-1
Att: 20,000 Fyfe 2, Johnstone, Burke (og)
1st Round (2nd leg)
Oct 1 vs Bohemians (a) 1-1 (agg. 5-2)
Att: 8,000 Johnstone
2nd Round (1st leg)
Oct 22 vs St. Etienne (a) 0-2
Att: 28,394
2nd Round (2nd leg)
Nov 5 vs St. Etienne (h) 1-2 (agg. 1-4)
Att: 45,000 MacDonald

1976/77 SEASON
1st Round (1st leg)
Sep 15 vs FC Zurich (h) 1-1
Att: 35,000 Parlane
1st Round (2nd leg)
Sep 29 vs FC Zurich (a) 0-1 (aggregate 1-2)
Att: 28,500

1978/79 SEASON
1st Round (1st leg)
Sep 13 vs Juventus (a) 0-1
Att: 60,000
1st Round (2nd leg)
Sep 27 vs Juventus (h) 2-0 (aggregate 2-1)
Att: 44,000 MacDonald, Smith
2nd Round (1st leg)
Oct 18 vs PSV Eindhoven (h) 0-0
Att: 44,000
2nd Round (2nd leg)
Nov 1 vs PSV Eindhoven (a) 3-2 (agg. 3-2)
Att: 28,000 MacDonald, Johnstone, Russell
Quarter-Final (1st leg)
Mar 6 vs Cologne (a) 0-1
Att: 40,000
Quarter-Final (2nd leg)
Mar 22 vs Cologne (h) 1-1 (aggregate 1-2)
Att: 44,000 McLean

1987/88 SEASON
1st Round (1st leg)
Sep 16 vs Dynamo Kiev (a) 0-1
Att: 100,000
1st Round (2nd leg)
Sep 30 vs Dynamo Kiev (h) 2-0 (agg. 2-1)
Att: 44,500 Falco, McCoist
2nd Round (1st leg)
Oct 21 vs Gornik Zabrze (h) 3-1
Att: 41,366 McCoist, Durrant, Falco
2nd Round (2nd leg)
Nov 4 vs Gornik Zabrze (a) 1-1 (agg. 4-2)
Att: 23,250 McCoist (pen)

Quarter-Final (1st leg)
Mar 2 vs Steaua Bucharest (a) 0-2
Att: 30,000
Quarter-Final (2nd leg)
Mar 16 vs Steaua Buch. (h) 2-1 (agg. 2-3)
Att: 44,000 Gough, McCoist (pen)

1989/90 SEASON
1st Round (1st leg)
Sep 13 vs Bayern Munich (h) 1-3
Att: 40,135 Walters (pen)
1st Round (2nd leg)
Sep 27 vs Bayern Munich (a) 0-0 (agg. 1)
Att: 43,000

1990/91 SEASON
1st Round (1st leg)
Sep 19 vs Valetta (a) 4-0
Att: 8,000 McCoist (pn), Hateley, Johnsto
1st Round (2nd leg)
Oct 2 vs Valetta (h) 6-0 (aggregate 10-0)
Att: 20,627 Dodds, Spencer, Johnston 3 (pen), McCoist
2nd Round (1st leg)
Oct 24 vs Red Star Belgrade (a) 0-3
Att: 82,000
2nd Round (2nd leg)
Nov 7 vs Red Star Belgrade (h) 1-1 (agg 1)
Att: 23,821 McCoist

1991/92 SEASON
1st Round (1st leg)
Sep 18 vs Sparta Prague (a) 0-1
Att: 11,053
1st Round (2nd leg)
Oct 2 vs Sparta Prague (h) 2-1 (aet) (agg)
Att: 34,260 McCall 2
Sparta Prague won on Away Goals

1992/93 SEASON
1st Round (1st leg)
Sep 16 vs Lyngby (h) 2-0
Att: 40,036 Hateley, Huistra
1st Round (2nd leg)
Sep 30 vs Lyngby (a) 1-0 (aggregate 3-0)
Att: 4,273 Durrant
2nd Round (1st leg)
Oct 21 vs Leeds United (h) 2-1
Att: 44,000 Lukic (og), McCoist
2nd Round (2nd leg)
Nov 4 vs Leeds United (a) 2-1 (agg. 4-2)
Att: 25,118 Hateley, McCoist
Group A, Game One
Nov 25 vs Marseille (h) 2-2
Att: 41,624 McSwegan, Hateley
Group A, Game Two (in Bochum)
Dec 9 vs CSKA Moscow (a) 1-0
Att: 9,000 Ferguson
Group A, Game Three
Mar 3 vs FC Brugge (a) 1-1
Att: 19,000 Huistra
Group A, Game Four
Mar 17 vs FC Brugge (h) 2-1
Att: 42,731 Durrant, Nisbet
Group A, Game Five
Apr 7 vs Marseille (a) 1-1
Att: 40,000 Durrant
Group A, Game Six
Apr 21 vs CSKA Moscow (h) 0-0
Att: 43,142

1993/94 SEASON
1st Round (1st leg)
Sep 15 vs Levski Sofia (h) 3-2
Att: 37,013 McPherson, Hateley 2
1st Round (2nd leg)
Sep 29 vs Levski Sofia (a) 1-2 (agg. 4-4)
Att: 50,000 Durrant
Levski Sofia win on Away Goals

1994/95 SEASON
Preliminary Round (1st leg)
Aug 10 vs AEK Athens (a) 0-2
Att: 35,000

Preliminary Round (2nd leg)
Aug 24 vs AEK Athens (h) 0-1 (agg. 0-3)
Att: 44,789

EUROPEAN CUP-WINNERS CUP

1971/72 SEASON
1st Round (1st leg)
Sep 15 vs Rennes (a) 1-1
Att: 20,000 Johnston

1st Round (2nd leg)
Sep 28 vs Rennes (h) 1-0 (aggregate 2-1)
Att: 40,000 Johnston

2nd Round (1st leg)
Oct 20 vs Sporting Lisbon (h) 3-2
Att: 40,000 Stein 2, Henderson

2nd Round (2nd leg)
Nov 3 vs Spor. Lisbon (a) 3-4 (aet) (agg. 6-6)
Att: 20,000 Stein 2, Henderson
Rangers won on Away Goals

Quarter-Final (1st leg)
Mar 8 vs Torino (a) 1-1
Att: 35,000 Johnston

Quarter-Final (2nd leg)
Mar 22 vs Torino (h) 1-0 (aggregate 2-1)
Att: 65,000 MacDonald

Semi-Final (1st leg)
Apr 5 vs Bayern Munich (a) 1-1
Att: 40,000 Zobel (og)

Semi-Final (2nd leg)
Apr 19 vs Bayern Munich (h) 2-0 (agg. 3-1)
Att: 80,000 Jardine, Parlane

FINAL (at Nuremburg)
May 24 vs Dynamo Moscow 3-2
Att: 35,000 Johnston 2, Stein

1973/74 SEASON
1st Round (1st leg)
Sep 19 vs Ankaragucu (a) 2-0
Att: 30,000 Conn, McLean

1st Round (2nd leg)
Oct 3 vs Ankaragucu (h) 4-0 (agg. 6-0)
Att: 20,000 Greig 2, O'Hara, Johnstone

2nd Round (1st leg)
Oct 24 vs Borussia Moen'gladbach (a) 0-3
Att: 33,000

2nd Round (2nd leg)
Nov 7 vs Boruss. Moench. (h) 3-2 (agg. 3-5)
Att: 40,000 Conn, Jackson, MacDonald

1977/78 SEASON
Preliminary Round (1st leg)
Aug 17 vs Young Boys Berne (h) 1-0
Att: 30,000 Greig

Preliminary Round (2nd leg)
Aug 31 vs Y. Boys Berne (a) 2-2 (agg. 3-2)
Att: 17,000 Johnstone, Smith

1st Round (1st leg)
Sep 14 vs Twente Enschede (h) 0-0
Att: 30,000

1st Round (2nd leg)
Sep 28 vs Twente Ensch. (a) 0-3 (agg. 0-3)
Att: 20,000

1979/80 SEASON
Preliminary Round (1st leg)
Aug 21 vs Lillestrom (h) 1-0
Att: 25,000 Smith

Preliminary Round (2nd leg)
Sep 5 vs Lillestrom (a) 2-0 (aggregate 3-0)
Att: 6,175 MacDonald, Johnston

1st Round (1st leg)
Sep 19 vs Fortuna Dusseldorf (h) 2-1
Att: 30,000 MacDonald, McLean

1st Round (2nd leg)
Oct 3 vs Fort. Dusseldorf (a) 0-0 (agg. 2-1)
Att: 40,000

2nd Round (1st leg)
Oct 24 vs Valencia (a) 1-1
Att: 45,000 McLean

2nd Round (2nd leg)
Nov 7 vs Valencia (h) 1-3 (aggregate 2-4)
Att: 36,000 Johnstone

1981/82 SEASON
1st Round (1st leg)
Sep 16 vs Dukla Prague (a) 0-3
Att: 22,500

1st Round (2nd leg)
Sep 30 vs Dukla Prague (h) 2-1 (agg. 2-4)
Att: 20,000 Bett, MacDonald

1983/84 SEASON
1st Round (1st leg)
Sep 14 vs Valetta (a) 8-0
*Att: 18,213 Paterson, McPherson 4, Mac-
Donald, Prytz 2*

1st Round (2nd leg)
Sep 28 vs Valetta (h) 10-0 (aggregate 18-0)
*Att: 10,423 Mitchell 2, MacDonald 3, Daw-
son, McKay, Davies 2, Redford*

2nd Round (1st leg)
Oct 19 vs Porto (h) 2-1
Att: 35,000 Clark, Mitchell

2nd Round (2nd leg)
Nov 2 vs Porto (a) 0-1 (aggregate 2-2)
Att: 60,000 Porto won on Away Goals

UEFA CUP
1970/71 SEASON
1st Round (1st leg)
Sep 16 vs Bayern Munich (a) 0-1
Att: 27,000

1st Round (2nd leg)
Sep 30 vs Bayern Munich (h) 1-1 (agg. 1-2)
Att: 70,000 Stein

1982/83 SEASON
1st Round (1st leg)
Sep 15 vs Borussia Dortmund (h) 0-0
Att: 54,000

1st Round (2nd leg)
Sep 29 vs Bor. Dortmund (a) 2-0 (agg. 2-0)
Att: 40,000 Cooper, Johnstone

2nd Round (1st leg)
Oct 20 vs Cologne (h) 2-1
Att: 35,000 Johnstone, McClelland

2nd Round (2nd leg)
Nov 3 vs Cologne (a) 0-5 (aggregate 2-6)
Att: 61,000

1984/85 SEASON
1st Round (1st leg)
Sep 18 vs Bohemians Dublin (a) 2-3
Att: 10,000 McCoist, McPherson

1st Round (2nd leg)
Oct 3 vs Bohemians (h) 2-0 (aggregate 4-3)
Att: 33,000 Paterson, Redford

2nd Round (1st leg)
Oct 24 vs Inter Milan (a) 0-3
Att: 65,000

2nd Round (2nd leg)
Nov 7 vs Inter Milan (h) 3-1 (aggregate 3-4)
Att: 33,000 Mitchell, Ferguson 2

1985/86 SEASON
1st Round (1st leg)
Sep 18 vs Osasuna (h) 1-0
Att: 29,479 Paterson

1st Round (2nd leg)
Oct 2 vs Osasuna (a) 0-2 (aggregate 1-2)
Att: 25,500

1986/87 SEASON
1st Round (1st leg)
Sep 17 vs Ilves (h) 4-0
Att: 27,436 Fleck 3, McCoist

1st Round (2nd leg)
Oct 1 vs Ilves (a) 0-2 (aggregate 4-2)
Att: 2,109

2nd Round (1st leg)
Oct 23 vs Boavista (h) 2-1
Att: 38,772 McPherson, McCoist

2nd Round (2nd leg)
Nov 4 vs Boavista (a) 1-0 (aggregate 3-1)
Att: 23,000 Ferguson

3rd Round (1st leg)
Nov 26 vs Borussia Moen'gladbach (a) 1-1
Att: 44,000 Durrant

3rd Round (2nd leg)
Dec 10 vs Bor. M'gladbach (a) 0-0 (agg. 1-1)
Att: 34,000 Borussia won on Away Goals

1988/89 SEASON
1st Round (1st leg)
Sep 7 vs GKS Katowice (h) 1-0
Att: 41,120 Walters

1st Round (2nd leg)
Oct 5 vs GKS Katowice (a) 4-2 (agg. 5-2)
Att: 35,000 Butcher 2, Durrant, Ferguson

2nd Round (1st leg)
Oct 26 vs Cologne (a) 0-2
Att: 42,000

2nd Round (2nd leg)
Nov 9 vs Cologne (h) 1-1 (aggregate 1-3)
Att: 42,204 Drinkell

1970-71 SEASON

FIRST DIVISION

Celtic	34	25	6	3	89	23	56
Aberdeen	34	24	6	4	68	18	54
St. Johnstone	34	19	6	9	59	44	44
Rangers	**34**	**16**	**9**	**9**	**58**	**34**	**41**
Dundee	34	14	10	10	53	45	38
Dundee United	34	14	8	12	53	54	36
Falkirk	34	13	9	12	46	53	35
Morton	34	13	8	13	44	44	34
Motherwell	34	13	8	13	43	47	34
Airdrieonians	34	13	8	13	60	65	34
Heart of Midlothian	34	13	7	14	41	40	33
Hibernian	34	10	10	14	47	53	30
Kilmarnock	34	10	8	16	43	67	28
Ayr United	34	9	8	17	37	54	26
Clyde	34	8	10	16	33	59	26
Dunfermline Athletic	34	6	11	17	44	56	23
St. Mirren	34	7	9	18	38	56	23
Cowdenbeath	34	7	3	24	33	77	17

1971-72 SEASON

FIRST DIVISION

Celtic	34	28	4	2	96	28	60
Aberdeen	34	21	8	5	80	26	50
Rangers	**34**	**21**	**2**	**11**	**71**	**38**	**44**
Hibernian	34	19	6	9	62	34	44
Dundee	34	14	13	7	59	38	41
Heart of Midlothian	34	13	13	8	53	49	39
Partick Thistle	34	12	10	12	53	54	34
St. Johnstone	34	12	8	14	52	58	32
Dundee United	34	12	7	15	55	70	31
Motherwell	34	11	7	16	49	69	29
Kilmarnock	34	11	6	17	49	64	28
Ayr United	34	9	10	15	40	58	28
Morton	34	10	7	17	46	52	27
Falkirk	34	10	7	17	44	60	27
Airdrieonians	34	7	12	15	44	76	26
East Fife	34	5	15	14	34	61	25
Clyde	34	7	10	17	33	66	24
Dunfermline Athletic	34	7	9	18	31	50	23

1972-73 SEASON

FIRST DIVISION

Celtic	34	26	5	3	93	28	57
Rangers	**34**	**26**	**4**	**4**	**74**	**30**	**56**
Hibernian	34	19	7	8	74	33	45
Aberdeen	34	16	11	7	61	34	43
Dundee	34	17	9	8	68	43	43
Ayr United	34	16	8	10	50	51	40
Dundee United	34	17	5	12	56	51	39
Motherwell	34	11	9	14	38	48	31
East Fife	34	11	8	15	46	54	30
Heart of Midlothian	34	12	6	16	39	50	30
St. Johnstone	34	10	9	15	52	67	29
Morton	34	10	8	16	47	53	28
Partick Thistle	34	10	8	16	40	53	28
Falkirk	34	7	12	15	38	56	26
Arbroath	34	9	8	17	39	63	26
Dumbarton	34	6	11	17	43	72	23
Kilmarnock	34	7	8	19	40	71	22
Airdrieonians	34	4	8	22	34	75	16

1973-74 SEASON

FIRST DIVISION

Celtic	34	23	7	4	82	27	53
Hibernian	34	20	9	5	75	42	49
Rangers	**34**	**21**	**6**	**7**	**67**	**34**	**48**
Aberdeen	34	13	16	5	46	26	42
Dundee	34	16	7	11	67	48	39
Heart of Midlothian	34	14	10	10	54	43	38
Ayr United	34	15	8	11	44	40	38
Dundee United	34	15	7	12	55	51	37
Motherwell	34	14	7	13	45	40	35
Dumbarton	34	11	7	16	43	58	29
Partick Thistle	34	9	10	15	33	46	28
St. Johnstone	34	9	10	15	41	60	28
Arbroath	34	10	7	17	52	69	27
Morton	34	8	10	16	37	49	26
Clyde	34	8	9	17	29	65	25
Dunfermline Athletic	34	8	8	18	43	65	24
East Fife	34	9	6	19	26	51	24
Falkirk	34	4	14	16	33	58	22

1974-75 SEASON

FIRST DIVISION

Rangers	**34**	**25**	**6**	**3**	**86**	**33**	**56**
Hibernian	34	20	9	5	69	37	49
Celtic	34	20	5	9	81	41	45
Dundee United	34	19	7	8	72	43	45
Aberdeen	34	16	9	9	66	43	41
Dundee	34	16	6	12	48	42	38
Ayr United	34	14	8	11	50	61	36
Heart of Midlothian	34	11	13	10	47	52	35
St. Johnstone	34	11	12	11	41	44	34
Motherwell	34	14	5	15	52	57	33
Airdrieonians	34	11	9	14	43	55	31
Kilmarnock	34	8	15	11	52	68	31
Partick Thistle	34	10	10	14	48	62	30
Dumbarton	34	7	10	17	44	55	24
Dunfermline Athletic	34	7	9	18	46	66	23
Clyde	34	6	10	18	40	63	22
Morton	34	6	10	18	31	62	22
Arbroath	34	5	7	22	34	66	17

1975-76 SEASON

PREMIER DIVISION

Rangers	**36**	**23**	**8**	**5**	**59**	**24**	**54**
Celtic	36	21	6	9	71	42	48
Hibernian	36	20	7	9	58	40	43
Motherwell	36	16	8	12	57	49	40
Heart of Midlothian	36	13	9	14	39	44	35
Ayr United	36	14	5	17	46	59	33
Aberdeen	36	11	10	15	49	50	32
Dundee United	36	12	8	16	46	48	32
Dundee	36	11	10	15	49	62	32
St. Johnstone	36	3	5	28	29	79	11

1976-77 SEASON

PREMIER DIVISION

Celtic	36	23	9	4	79	39	55
Rangers	**36**	**18**	**10**	**8**	**62**	**37**	**46**
Aberdeen	36	16	11	9	56	42	43
Dundee United	36	16	9	11	54	45	41
Partick Thistle	36	11	13	12	40	44	35
Hibernian	36	8	18	10	34	35	34
Motherwell	36	10	12	14	57	60	32
Ayr United	36	11	8	17	44	68	30
Heart of Midlothian	36	7	13	16	49	66	27
Kilmarnock	36	4	9	23	32	71	17

1977-78 SEASON

PREMIER DIVISION

Rangers	**36**	**24**	**7**	**5**	**76**	**39**	**55**
Aberdeen	36	22	9	5	68	29	53
Dundee United	36	16	8	12	42	32	40
Hibernian	36	15	7	14	51	43	37
Celtic	36	15	6	15	63	54	36
Motherwell	36	13	7	16	45	52	33
Partick Thistle	36	14	5	17	52	64	33
St. Mirren	36	11	8	17	52	63	30
Ayr United	36	9	6	21	36	68	24
Clydebank	36	6	7	23	23	64	19

1978-79 SEASON

PREMIER DIVISION

Celtic	36	21	6	9	61	37	48
Rangers	**36**	**18**	**9**	**9**	**52**	**35**	**45**
Dundee United	36	18	8	10	56	37	44
Aberdeen	36	13	14	9	59	36	40
Hibernian	36	12	13	11	44	48	37
St. Mirren	36	15	6	15	45	41	36
Morton	36	12	12	12	52	53	36
Partick Thistle	36	13	8	15	42	39	34
Heart of Midlothian	36	8	7	21	49	71	23
Motherwell	36	5	7	24	33	86	17

1979-80 SEASON

PREMIER DIVISION

Aberdeen	36	19	10	7	68	36	48
Celtic	36	18	11	7	61	38	47
St. Mirren	36	15	12	9	56	49	42
Dundee United	36	12	13	11	43	30	37
Rangers	**36**	**15**	**7**	**14**	**50**	**46**	**37**
Morton	36	14	8	14	51	46	36
Partick Thistle	36	11	14	11	43	47	36
Kilmarnock	36	11	11	14	36	52	33
Dundee	36	10	6	20	47	73	26
Hibernian	36	6	6	24	29	67	18

1980-81 SEASON

PREMIER DIVISION

Celtic	36	26	4	6	84	37	56
Aberdeen	36	19	11	6	61	26	49
Rangers	**36**	**16**	**12**	**8**	**60**	**32**	**44**
St. Mirren	36	18	8	10	56	47	44
Dundee United	36	17	9	10	66	42	43
Partick Thistle	36	10	10	16	32	48	30
Airdrieonians	36	10	9	17	36	55	29
Morton	36	10	8	18	36	58	28
Kilmarnock	36	5	9	22	23	65	19
Heart of Midlothian	36	6	6	24	27	71	18

1981-82 SEASON

PREMIER DIVISION

Celtic	36	24	7	5	79	33	55
Aberdeen	36	23	7	6	71	29	53
Rangers	**36**	**16**	**11**	**9**	**57**	**45**	**43**
Dundee United	36	15	10	11	61	38	40
St. Mirren	36	14	9	13	49	52	37
Hibernian	36	11	14	11	48	40	36
Morton	36	9	12	15	31	54	30
Dundee	36	11	4	21	46	72	26
Partick Thistle	36	6	10	20	35	59	22
Airdrieonians	36	5	8	23	31	76	18

1982-83 SEASON

PREMIER DIVISION

Dundee United	36	24	8	4	90	35	56
Celtic	36	25	5	6	90	36	55
Aberdeen	36	25	5	6	76	24	55
Rangers	**36**	**13**	**12**	**11**	**52**	**41**	**38**
St. Mirren	36	11	12	13	47	51	34
Dundee	36	9	11	16	42	53	29
Hibernian	36	11	7	18	35	51	29
Motherwell	36	11	5	20	39	73	27
Morton	36	6	8	22	30	74	20
Kilmarnock	36	3	11	22	28	91	17

1983-84 SEASON

PREMIER DIVISION

Aberdeen	36	25	7	4	78	21	57
Celtic	36	21	8	7	80	41	50
Dundee United	36	18	11	7	67	39	47
Rangers	**36**	**15**	**12**	**9**	**53**	**41**	**42**
Heart of Midlothian	36	10	16	10	38	47	36
St. Mirren	36	9	14	13	55	59	32
Hibernian	36	12	7	17	45	55	31
Dundee	36	11	5	20	50	74	27
St. Johnstone	36	10	3	23	36	81	23
Motherwell	36	4	7	25	31	75	15

1984-85 SEASON

PREMIER DIVISION

Aberdeen	36	27	5	4	89	26	59
Celtic	36	22	8	6	77	30	52
Dundee United	36	20	7	9	67	33	47
Rangers	**36**	**13**	**12**	**11**	**47**	**38**	**38**
St. Mirren	36	17	4	15	51	56	38
Dundee	36	15	7	14	48	50	37
Heart of Midlothian	36	13	5	18	47	64	31
Hibernian	36	10	7	19	38	61	27
Dumbarton	36	6	7	23	29	64	19
Morton	36	5	2	29	29	100	12

1985-86 SEASON

PREMIER DIVISION

Celtic	36	20	10	6	67	38	50
Heart of Midlothian	36	20	10	6	59	33	50
Dundee United	36	18	11	7	59	31	47
Aberdeen	36	16	12	8	62	31	44
Rangers	**36**	**13**	**9**	**14**	**53**	**45**	**35**
Dundee	36	14	7	15	45	51	35
St. Mirren	36	13	5	18	42	63	31
Hibernian	36	11	6	19	49	63	28
Motherwell	36	7	6	23	33	66	20
Clydebank	36	6	8	22	29	77	20

1986-87 SEASON
PREMIER DIVISION

Rangers	44	31	7	6	85	23	69
Celtic	44	27	9	8	90	41	63
Dundee United	44	24	12	8	66	36	60
Aberdeen	44	21	16	7	63	29	58
Heart of Midlothian	44	21	14	9	64	43	56
Dundee	44	18	12	14	74	57	48
St. Mirren	44	12	12	20	36	51	36
Motherwell	44	11	12	21	43	64	34
Hibernian	44	10	13	21	44	70	33
Falkirk	44	8	10	26	31	70	26
Clydebank	44	6	12	26	35	93	24
Hamilton Acad.	44	6	9	29	39	93	21

1987-88 SEASON
PREMIER DIVISION

Celtic	44	30	10	4	78	24	70
Heart of Midlothian	44	23	16	5	74	32	62
Rangers	44	26	8	10	85	34	60
Aberdeen	44	20	17	7	55	26	57
Dundee United	44	15	15	14	51	50	45
Dundee	44	18	7	19	71	63	43
Hibernian	44	12	19	13	41	43	43
Motherwell	44	13	10	21	37	56	36
St. Mirren	44	10	15	19	41	64	35
Falkirk	44	11	11	22	42	74	33
Dunfermline Athletic	44	9	10	25	45	81	28
Morton	44	3	10	31	27	100	16

1988-89 SEASON
PREMIER DIVISION

Rangers	36	26	4	6	62	26	56
Aberdeen	36	18	14	4	51	25	50
Celtic	36	21	4	11	66	44	46
Dundee United	36	16	12	8	44	26	44
Hibernian	36	13	9	14	37	36	35
Heart of Midlothian	36	9	13	14	35	42	31
St. Mirren	36	11	7	18	39	55	29
Dundee	36	9	10	17	34	48	28
Motherwell	36	7	13	16	35	44	27
Hamilton Acad.	36	6	2	28	19	76	14

1989-90 SEASON
PREMIER DIVISION

Rangers	36	20	11	5	48	19	51
Aberdeen	36	17	10	9	56	33	44
Heart of Midlothian	36	16	12	8	54	35	44
Dundee United	36	11	13	12	36	39	35
Celtic	36	10	14	12	37	37	34
Motherwell	36	11	12	13	43	47	34
Hibernian	36	12	10	14	34	41	34
Dunfermline Athletic	36	11	8	17	37	50	30
St. Mirren	36	10	10	16	28	48	30
Dundee	36	5	14	17	41	65	24

1990-91 SEASON
PREMIER DIVISION

Rangers	36	24	7	5	62	23	55
Aberdeen	36	22	9	5	62	27	53
Celtic	36	17	7	12	52	38	41
Dundee United	36	17	7	12	41	29	41
Heart of Midlothian	36	14	7	15	48	55	35
Motherwell	36	12	9	15	51	50	33
St. Johnstone	36	11	9	16	41	54	31
Dunfermline Athletic	36	8	11	17	38	61	27
Hibernian	36	6	13	17	24	51	25
St. Mirren	36	5	9	22	28	59	19

1991-92 SEASON
PREMIER DIVISION

Rangers	44	33	6	5	101	31	72
Heart of Midlothian	44	27	9	8	60	37	63
Celtic	44	26	10	8	88	42	62
Dundee United	44	19	13	12	66	50	51
Hibernian	44	16	17	11	53	45	49
Aberdeen	44	17	14	13	55	42	48
Airdrieonians	44	13	10	21	50	70	36
St. Johnstone	44	13	10	21	52	73	36
Falkirk	44	12	11	21	54	73	35
Motherwell	44	10	14	20	43	61	34
St. Mirren	44	6	12	26	33	73	24
Dunfermline Athletic	44	4	10	30	22	80	18

1992-93 SEASON
PREMIER DIVISION

Rangers	44	33	7	4	97	35	73
Aberdeen	44	27	10	7	87	36	64
Celtic	44	24	12	8	68	41	60
Dundee United	44	19	9	16	56	49	47
Heart of Midlothian	44	15	14	15	46	51	44
St. Johnstone	44	10	19	15	51	66	39
Hibernian	44	12	13	19	54	64	37
Partick Thistle	44	12	12	20	50	71	36
Motherwell	44	12	12	20	46	61	36
Dundee	44	11	12	21	48	68	34
Falkirk	44	11	7	26	60	86	29
Airdrieonians	44	6	17	21	35	70	29

1994-95 SEASON
PREMIER DIVISION

Rangers	36	20	9	7	60	35	69
Motherwell	36	14	12	10	50	50	54
Hibernian	36	12	17	7	49	37	53
Celtic	36	11	18	7	39	33	51
Falkirk	36	12	12	12	48	47	48
Heart of Midlothian	36	12	7	17	44	51	43
Kilmarnock	36	11	10	15	40	48	43
Partick Thistle	36	10	13	13	40	50	43
Aberdeen	36	10	11	15	43	46	41
Dundee United	36	9	9	18	40	56	36

1993-94 SEASON
PREMIER DIVISION

Rangers	44	22	14	8	74	41	58
Aberdeen	44	17	21	6	58	36	55
Motherwell	44	20	14	10	58	43	54
Celtic	44	15	20	9	51	38	50
Hibernian	44	16	15	13	53	48	47
Dundee United	44	11	20	13	47	48	42
Heart of Midlothian	44	11	20	13	37	43	42
Kilmarnock	44	12	16	16	36	45	40
Partick Thistle	44	12	16	16	46	57	40
St. Johnstone	44	10	20	14	35	47	40
Raith Rovers	44	6	19	19	46	76	31
Dundee	44	8	13	23	42	57	29